Cameos

Cameos

A Pocket Guide with Values
Revised & Expanded 3rd Edition

Monica Lynn Clements and Patricia Rosser Clements

Schiffer Publishing Ltd

4880 Lower Valley Road, Atglen, Pennsylvania 19310

Other Schiffer Books by Monica Lynn Clements & Patricia Rosser Clements:

Avon Collectible Fashion Jewelry and Awards, 0-7643-0523-9, $29.95
Sarah Coventry Jewelry: An Unauthorized Guide for Collectors, 0-7643-0686-3, $29.95
Pocket Guide to Occupied Japan, 0-7643-0728-2, $16.95
Cobalt Blue Glass, 0-7643-1258-8, $24.95
The Pocket Guide to Green Depression Era Glass, 0-7643-1535-8, $16.95

Other Schiffer Books on Related Subjects:

Glass in Jewelry, 0-7643-0532-8, $29.95
Rhinestones! A Collector's Handbook and Price Guide, 0-7643-1751-2, $16.95
Collecting Plastic Jewelry: A Handbook and Price Guide, 0-7643-0024-5, $16.95

● ●

Revised price guide: 2011
Copyright © 1999, 2003 & 2011 by Monica Lynn Clements & Patricia Rosser Clements
Library of Congress Control Number: 2010941143

Designed by Bonnie M. Walleigh
Type set in Lydian Csv BT/Lydian BT

ISBN: 978-0-7643-3807-6
Printed in China

Schiffer Books are available at special discounts for bulk purchases for sales promotions or premiums. Special editions, including personalized covers, corporate imprints, and excerpts can be created in large quantities for special needs. For more information contact the publisher:

Published by Schiffer Publishing Ltd.
4880 Lower Valley Road
Atglen, PA 19310
Phone: (610) 593-1777; Fax: (610) 593-2002
E-mail: Info@schifferbooks.com

For the largest selection of fine reference books on this and related subjects, please visit our web site at: www.schifferbooks.com We are always looking for people to write books on new and related subjects. If you have an idea for a book please contact us at the above address.

This book may be purchased from the publisher. Include $5.00 for shipping. Please try your bookstore first. You may write for a free catalog.

In Europe, Schiffer books are distributed by
Bushwood Books
6 Marksbury Ave.
Kew Gardens
Surrey TW9 4JF England
Phone: 44 (0) 20 8392 8585; Fax: 44 (0) 20 8392 9876
E-mail: info@bushwoodbooks.co.uk
Website: www.bushwoodbooks.co.uk

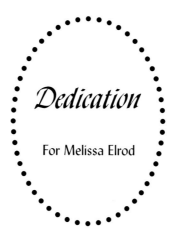

Dedication

For Melissa Elrod

Acknowledgments

Our thanks to each contributor who shared his or her cameo for this book. A special thank you to Frank and Dorothy Everts, Melissa Elrod, Teresa J. Rogers, Chris Terry, and Mary Liles. As always, we thank Mary G. Moon and Kenneth L. Surratt, Jr. for their enthusiasm and diligence.

Contents

Introduction

In our first book, *Cameos: Classical to Costume*, we presented a large array of cameos. We continue to be amazed at the large variety of cameo jewelry available. Cameos are truly an art form, and in the following pages, you, the reader, will find the evidence of this. We have included something that will appeal to everyone from the formal carvings of the nineteenth century to the colorful and informal plastic and glass examples of molded relief jewelry. This guide serves as a companion to our first book. The advantage of a pocket guide is the size and versatility for those who wish to carry a reference on their search for cameos.

The purpose of this book is not to set prices, but to be a guide. The prices of cameos reflect the combined experience of both authors in collecting and dealing in antique and collectible jewelry. They are representative of the range of values observed throughout the United States and Europe.

History

No other jewelry has been more recognizable than the cameo. Although the style of the cameo has changed, it has continued to grow in popularity. The traditional definition of a cameo is a piece of jewelry that is carved in relief. This definition includes stone and shell, but cameos have been fashioned out of other materials such as coral, Gutta-percha, bog oak, ivory, lava, and mother-of-pearl. The meaning of this definition can be expanded to include molded relief jewelry in glass or plastic.

Left: Enlarged view of gold locket with prong set shell cameo depicting woman's portrait, c.1940s. $195-230.
Below: Enlarged view of gold and enameled locket with onyx cameo depicting woman's portrait, c.1940s. $230-255.

Cameo lockets *courtesy of Teresa J. Rogers.*

Opposite page:
Top left: Stone cameo depicting Dionysus (Bacchante), god of wine and fertility, with grape leaves in hair, c.1840s. $95-125.
Top center: Stone cameo depicting woman's portrait, c.1840s. $195-225.
Top right: Shell cameo depicting Artemis (Diana) with crescent moon in hair, c.1860s. $75-95.
Bottom left: Shell cameo depicting Hera, wife of Zeus, wearing diadem, c. 1840. $95-125.
Bottom center: Stone cameo, depicts Artemis (Diana) with crescent moon in hair, c.1860s. $195-225.
Bottom right: Stone cameo depicting woman's portrait, c.1860s. $125-150.

Cameos *courtesy of Frank and Dorothy Everts.*

Top: Brooch with prong set stone cameo depicting Hera, wife of Zeus, wearing diadem, set in gold frame, c. 1820s. $450-500.

Bottom: Pendant necklace with shell cameo depicting Hera, wife of Zeus, wearing diadem, set in gold frame with two pearls and moonstones attached to necklace, c.1820s. $500-600.

Cameos courtesy of Teresa J. Rogers.

Gold filled bracelet with coral cameo depicting woman's portrait, 1910. $1800-2000.
Courtesy of Teresa J. Rogers.

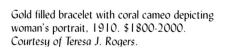

Above right: 9KG stickpin with coral cameo; depicts woman's portrait, c.1890s. $235-260.
Above left: Brooch with coral cameo depicting woman's portrait, set in gold frame, c.1890s. $450-500.

Coral cameos courtesy of Pat Constantino.

Left: Bog oak brooch with bird and flowers motif, c.1880s. $295-325.
Center: Gutta-percha brooch with floral design, c.1880s. $350-400.
Right: Gutta-percha pendant with floral motif, c.1880s. $350-400.

Brooches and pendant courtesy of Melissa Elrod.

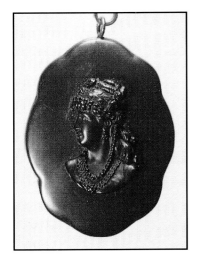

Brooch with prong set jet cameo depicting Psyche, bride of Cupid, with butterfly wing in hair, set in gold metal frame, c.1890s. $295-325. *Courtesy of Nancy Rainey Granich.*

Gutta-percha pendant depicting woman, c.1890s. $450-475. *Courtesy of Melissa Elrod.*

Glass cameo depicting Psyche, bride of Cupid, attached to jet background, set in gold metal frame with leaf motif, c.1890s. $325-350. *Courtesy of Teresa J. Rogers.*

13

Top left: Cameo habillé locket/pendant depicting Demeter (Ceres), goddess of the harvest, with four glass stones in wreath shape on head and wheat, c.1890s. $250-275.
Top center: Metal cameo habillé stickpin depicting woman with black stone, c.1940s. $175-195.
Top right: Metal brooch with portrait of man, c.1960s. $195-225.
Center left: Silver metal brooch depicting Mardi Gras motif, c.1920s. $300-400.
Bottom center: Gold metal brooch with floral motif and portrait of woman, c.1940s. $195-225.

Metal cameos courtesy of Melissa Elrod.

Simulated pearl necklace with jet cameo clasp depicting woman, c.1950s. $195-225.
Courtesy of Chaney Raley.

Top: Earrings with white on black plastic cameos depicting woman adorned with flowers surrounded by simulated seed pearls, c.1960s. $40-50.
Center: Gold metal bracelet with three white on black plastic prong set cameos depicting Psyche, bride of Cupid, with butterfly wing in hair surrounded by simulated seed pearls, c.1960s. $65-75.
Bottom: Velvet choker with three white on black plastic prong set cameos depicting Psyche, bride of Cupid, with butterfly wing in hair, surrounded by simulated seed pearls joined by gold metal chains, c.1960s. $65-75.

Cameos courtesy of Kenneth L. Surratt, Jr.

Related to the cameo is the intaglio. An intaglio is the opposite of the cameo, and the carver works below the surface to create a unique type of jewelry. Unlike the cameo, the early intaglios have a purpose. For example, they were once used to mark property. Today, they are worn as jewelry, and have become quite popular. A similarity that the intaglio shares with the cameo is that the intaglio can be found in a variety of materials.

While most people equate the cameo with shell, other materials preceded shell as the medium chosen by carvers. Stone provided artisans with a means to use many layers to create a detailed and sometimes three-dimensional carving. Carved gemstones reached the height of fashion during the

Brooch with stone cameo depicting woman set in gold frame, c.1860s. $1200-1500. *Courtesy of Mary Liles.*

15

eighteenth century. Women wore parures of carved gems that sparkled in salons of the day.

A practice used by those who produced cameos was to take plaster of paris molds of carved gemstones. The plaster molds provided a record of noted cameo collections. Today, these plaster replicas offer an interesting insight into the motifs that interested cameo enthusiasts of the past.

Enlarged view of plaster of Paris cast depicting Caesar, c.1750s. *Courtesy of Mary Liles.*

Enlarged view of plaster of paris cast depicting sixteenth century
man, c.1750s. *Courtesy of Mary Liles.*

Pages 18 and 19: An assortment of plaster casts illustrate the religious, mythological, and animal
motifs that appealed to cameo enthusiasts in the eighteenth century, c. 1750s. *Courtesy of Frank
and Dorothy Everts.*

18

At one time, only the wealthy could afford cameos, but glass paste offered a means for the masses to enjoy cameo jewelry. The use of glass paste goes as far back as the days of the Romans. Glass cameo jewelry experienced a resurgence of popularity in the eighteenth century through the work of James Tassie (1735-1799). He developed the practice of making molds of collections and then producing glass paste jewelry that emulated the look of carved gems. Glass continues to be a common medium for cameos today and can be found in many colorful costume jewelry pieces.

The use of shell began when carvers wanted a quick way to fashion a design and discovered that shell provided a soft material that was easy to carve. The less formal nature of the shell cameo appealed to consumers. For example, Empress Josephine liked to wear shell cameos everyday and made them popular in France. Their popularity spread from France to England, where Queen Victoria wore shell cameos and gave them as gifts.

During the Victorian Era, archaeological discoveries made at Pompeii provided rich colored lava for cameos. The consistency of lava made it perfect for producing highly detailed, three-dimensional carvings. Nineteenth century women who traveled to Italy on the Grand Tour found lava cameos to be the perfect souvenir because of the compact size. This type of cameo became a status symbol for ladies of the day to signify that they had traveled abroad. Many examples of the fine carvings exist today. The material is not as sturdy as shell or stone and breaks easily; yet the high relief in the surviving cameos is stunning. If a cameo is lava, one can say with a great deal of certainty that it originated in the 1800s. For more examples of this art form, please see the extensive chapter on lava cameos in our first book, *Cameos: Classical to Costume*.

Opposite page:
Top left and right: Lava cameos depicting cherubs in motion, c.1840s. $140-165.
Center: Lava cameo depicting seated cherub, c.1840s. $150-175.
Bottom left: Intaglio depicting Ares, god of war, c. 1860s. $175-195.
Bottom center: Wooden cameo depicting woman's portrait, c.1860s. $95-125.
Bottom right: Wooden intaglio depicting (Ceres) Demeter, goddess of the harvest, c. 1850s. $95-125.

Cameos courtesy of Frank and Dorothy Everts.

Above: Black lava cameo brooch depicting woman set in gold metal frame with rope design, c.1860s.
Right: Lava cameo brooch/pendant with portrait design set in gold frame, c.1860s.

Lava cameos courtesy of Jackie McDonald.

The popularity of the cameo meant it was incorporated into everyday life. By using the cameo as a symbol of his reign in France, Napoleon heightened the trend by commissioning furniture to be made of and adorned with cameos. Napoleon brought carvers from Italy to Paris to produce cameo jewelry for men and women. As Victorians made cameos popular in England, cameos began to take interesting forms. For example, cameos found their way onto metal, jasparware, and wooden buttons of the Victorian Era. With something as simple as a button, the masses could enjoy the styles popular in cameo jewelry such as the mythological motifs, floral motifs, and portraiture.

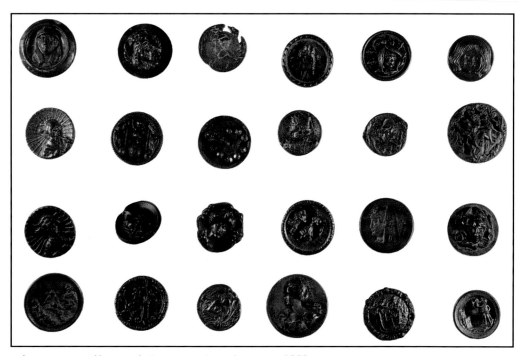

An assortment of buttons depicting portraits and scenes, c. 1860s.
Courtesy of Garden Gate Antiques, Texarkana, Arkansas.

Oppostie page :
Top: An assortment of buttons in metal, Gutta-percha, and jasparware, c. 1860s.
Courtesy of Garden Gate Antiques.

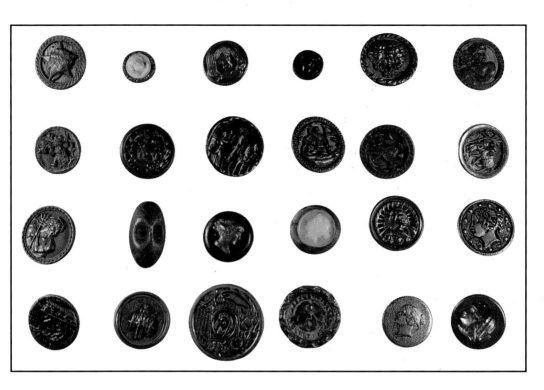

An assortment of metal buttons depicting portraits and mythological motifs, c. 1860s.
Courtesy of Garden Gate Antiques.

An assortment of metal buttons depicting mythological motifs, c.1860s.
Courtesy of Garden Gate Antiques.

An assortment of metal buttons depicting mythological motifs, c. 1860s.
Courtesy of Garden Gate Antiques.

Resourceful artisans looked to other materials to create cameos. Gutta-percha cameos appeared in the mourning jewelry of the nineteenth century. Carvers turned to ivory to create various designs that did not always bear the traditional portrait of the anonymous woman. Celluloid appeared in the late 1890s, although this material gave way to Lucite and the plastic in cameos we know today.

Far left: Gutta-percha locket/pendant with portrait of woman, c.1860s. $350-400.
Left: Gutta-percha locket/pendant with floral motif, c.1860s. $300-350.

Gutta-percha lockets courtesy of Melissa Elrod.

Above: White on black celluloid cameo pendant depicting woman's portrait, c.1890s. $295-325.
Left: Prong set white on black celluloid cameo depicting woman's portrait, set in gold metal frame, c.1890s. $395-425.

Cameos courtesy of Teresa J. Rogers.

After World War II, the emergence of costume jewelry created a new demand for cameos. This need has produced cameos in different materials that collectors enjoy today. While plastic cameos are numerous, the traditional shell cameo still provides elegance, and glass cameos in different colors have found popularity with costume jewelry enthusiasts.

Left: Sterling silver gold wash screw back earrings with shell cameos depicting woman's portrait, 1941. $95-125.
Top center: Sterling silver earrings with shell cameos depicting woman's portrait surrounded by marcasites, c.1980s. $50-60.
Bottom center: Gold filigree earrings with shell cameos depicting woman's portrait with glass stones, c.1930s. $150-175.
Right: Florenza gold metal earrings with prong set cameos depicting woman's portrait, c.1940s. $195-225.

Earrings courtesy of Teresa J. Rogers.

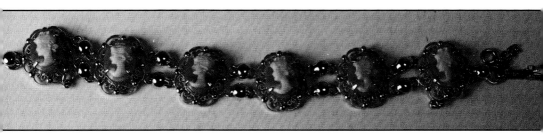

Alice Caviness bracelet with six shell cameos depicting woman's portrait, set in 1/20 12KG frame. $900-1200. *Courtesy of Darlene Dixon.*

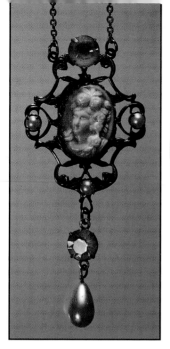

Far left: Pendant with glass cameo depicting woman's portrait, set in gold metal with two rhinestones, two simulated pearls, and simulated pearl drop, c.1940s. $225-275. Left. Loose milk glass cameo depicting muse, c.1880s. $195-225.

Cameos courtesy of Melissa Elrod.

Popular Motifs

The portrait is the subject most associated with the cameo. In the past, a portrait on a cameo signified an actual person's likeness, such as a ruler, scholar, philosopher, or other important person of the day. For women traveling on the grand tour, a prized souvenir was a cameo in which a carver fashioned a woman's likeness. Over the years, the woman's portrait has evolved. As this depiction has become more mass produced, the portrait most common is the anonymous woman's likeness.

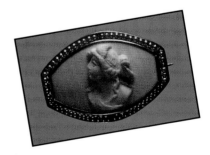

Above: Shell brooch depicting woman's portrait, set in gold frame with seed pearls (two missing), c.1820s. $400-500. Left. Shell brooch/pendant depicting woman's portrait, set in gold frame, c.1820s. $900-1200.

Cameos courtesy of Teresa J. Rogers.

A variation on the anonymous woman's portrait is the cameo habillé. In the late nineteenth century, carvers began to create portraits in which small diamonds enhanced the carved jewelry in the portrait. Other cameo habillés can be found with such additions as glass stones or even metal instead of diamonds. A cameo habillé is a distinctive piece of jewelry popular with those collectors who want an alternative to the traditional cameo.

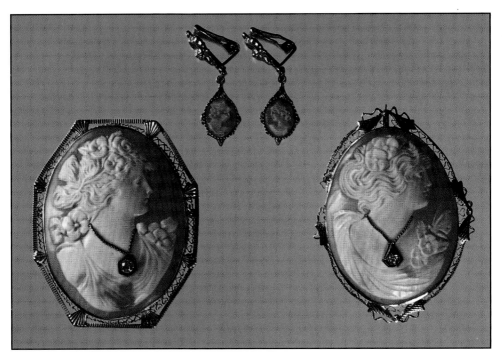

Left: Shell cameo habillé brooch/pendant depicting Flora, goddess of flowers, set in 14K white gold frame, c. 1890s. $1500-2000.
Top center: Clip-on earrings with shell cameos depicting woman's portrait, set in gold metal frames, c.1920s. $225-275.
Right: Shell cameo habillé pendant depicting Psyche, bride of Cupid, with butterfly on shoulder, set in white gold frame with some damage to the left side, c.1920s. $1500-1600.

Cameos courtesy of Angelia Jones.

A less common motif is the religious scene. Rebecca at the Well represents a popular setting for cameos of the Victorian Era. While the Rebecca at the Well scenes vary according to the carver's design, each contains a woman, a well, and a house. Other subjects can be found on mourning brooches to signify a person's journey to heaven. Carvers have portrayed a variety of religious figures and scenes on cameos. For example, a mother-of-pearl cameo contains a motif taken from the Garden of Eden.

Enlarged view of rectangular shell cameo depicting the Rebecca at the Well scene, set in twisted gold frame, c.1860s. $1200-1500.

The mythological motif has endured in popularity since the days of Alexander the Great. The archaeological discoveries of the nineteenth century intensified the Victorian's interest in Roman motifs. Among the most common subjects of the Victorian Era were Psyche, the bride of Cupid, with a butterfly wing in her hair or on her shoulder; Artemis (Diana), the goddess of the hunt, with a crescent moon in her hair; and Demeter (Ceres), goddess of the harvest, with a stalk of wheat. Additionally, Dionysus (Bacchus), the god of wine and fertility, was a frequent subject, appearing with grapes and grape leaves in his hair. Related to the Dionysus (Bacchus) motif was the Bacchante maiden, a follower of Dionysus (Bacchus), adorned with grapes and grape leaves. The Three Muses also have been depicted on many cameos. These and other gods and goddesses have found their way onto creations of the twentieth century.

Loose cameo depicting Artemis (Diana), goddess of the hunt, with crescent moon in hair, c.1860s. $300-400. *Courtesy of Out 'n Back Antiques, Bismarck, Arkansas.*

Enlarged coral cameo brooch depicting Bacchante maiden, follower of Dionysus (Bacchus), god of wine and fertility, with grapes and grape leaves in hair, set in gold frame with four pearls, 1.25", c.1820s. $900-1200. *Courtesy of Teresa J. Rogers.*

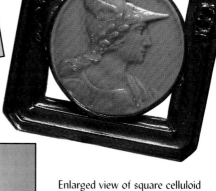

Enlarged view of square celluloid brooch depicting Hermes (Mercury), messenger for the gods, with winged hat, set in gold metal frame, 1.75", c.1890s. $195-225. *Courtesy of Martha Watkins.*

Shell cameo brooch with mythological scene depicting muses, set in gold frame adorned with flowers, c.1840s. $3000-4000. *Courtesy of Melissa Elrod.*

Left: Brooch with white on blue plastic cameo depicting Three Muses set in silver metal frame, c.1960s. $75-95.
Right: Pendant with plastic cameo depicting Artemis (Diana), goddess of the hunt, with crescent moon in hair and bow set in gold metal frame, c.1970s. $70-80.

Cameos courtesy of Great Finds and Designs, Texarkana, Texas.

Brooch with Wedgwood style white on blue plastic cameo depicting Apollo with lyre, set in twisted silver metal frame, c.1980s. $50-60.
Courtesy of Great Finds and Designs.

Cameos of today contain the designs of the past. Carvers in Italy continue to produce cameos using the old-fashioned method of carving, along with the popular motifs of the generalized woman and the mythological motifs. In scenes, carvers have chosen to portray women in motion. While mythological motifs provide a welcomed alternative for the collector, the anonymous woman remains prevalent.

Shell cameo; depicts Zeus with one of his lovers, c.1980s. $350-400. Courtesy of Chaney Raley.

How To Date A Cameo

Dating a cameo can pose a challenge for the collector. Knowing something about the provenance of a piece is extremely helpful. Even without any prior knowledge of a piece, the collector can act as a detective and learn much from the cameo.

A key to determine the age is to study the features of the portrait on the cameo. Roman women wearing no jewelry are indicative of the first half of the 1800s. Women traveling to Italy during the Victorian Era rejected the likeness of the Roman woman. They insisted that cameos portray more realistic looking women with necks that were not so thick, upswept hair, and jewelry. Short curls mean the cameo is from the 1920s or 1930s.

The nose also provides a clue about the age of a cameo. A long Roman nose means the cameo probably originated in the first half of the 1800s. During the Victorian Era, depictions of the nose turned it slightly upwards. By the 1920s, noses on cameos appeared pert.

To discern between the many materials from which cameos are made, the best solution is to handle cameos made from different materials. The more experience one gains, the easier it is to learn the feel of the different materials. Tapping a cameo lightly against one's teeth is a way to become more proficient in determining the difference between stone, shell, or plastic.

The more time a collector spends with cameos, the more he or she will learn. And with the wide variety of cameos and their history made available, hours of fascinating study await the collector. Part of the fun is acting as a detective to discern information about a cameo. Cameos remain a special and distinctive art form, and they continue to grow in popularity.

Ivory

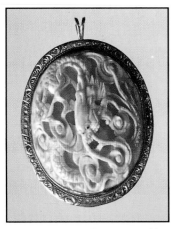

Ivory cameo pendant set in gold metal frame, c.1920s. $225-275. *Courtesy of Mary Liles.*

Ivory frame with ivory cameo depicting man, c.1920s. $450-475. *Courtesy of Melissa Elrod.*

Above: Ivory cameo pendant with portrait, c.1960s. $225-275.
Right: Ivory pendant with deer motif, c.1950s. $195-225.

Ivory jewelry courtesy of Melissa Elrod.

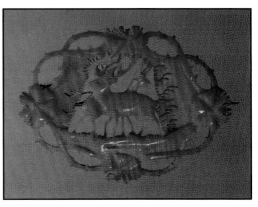

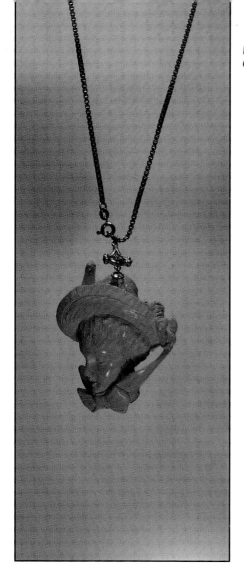

Man wearing hat, c.1890s. $225-325.
Courtesy of Melissa Elrod.

The rear view of an ivory cameo
depicting man wearing hat.

35

Lava

Gray cameo depicting Ceres (Demeter), goddess of the harvest, with diadem made of wheat, c. 1840s. $250-275.

Opposite page:
Top left: Small gray cameo depicting portrait of cherub, c.1840s.
Top center: Large brown cameo depicting Dionysus (Bacchus), god of wine and fertility, with grapes and grape leaves in hair, c.1840s.
Top right: Small brown cameo depicting Apollo with laurel wreath, c. 1840s.
Top right: Three-dimensional brown cameo depicting portrait of woman, c.1840s.
Upper left: Small brown cameo depicting high relief portrait of Dionysus (Bacchus), god of wine and fertility, with grapes and grape leaves in hair, c.1840s.
Upper center left: Large gray cameo with a three-dimensional portrait depicting Artemis (Diana), goddess of the hunt, with animals and crescent moon, c. 1830s.
Upper center left and right: Pair of small brown cameos depicting floral motif, c.1840s.
Center: Large brown cameo depicting Dionysus (Bacchus) with pine cones in hair, c. 1840s.
Upper center right: Beige cameo depicting three-dimensional portrait of woman, c.1840s.
Center left and right: Pair of small brown cameos depicting portraits of cupid in profile, c.1840s.
Center left: Black cameo with portrait of bearded man with damage to cameo on left and right, c.1840s.
Lower center: Beige cameo depicting three-dimensional portrait of Flora, goddess of flowers, c.1840s.
Center right: Black cameo depicting portrait in profile of angel, c.1840s.
Center right: Small cameo depicting portrait in profile of woman, c.1850s.
Lower left: Beige cameo depicting portrait in profile of angel, c.1840s.
Lower left: Cameo depicting three-dimensional portrait of Artemis (Diana), goddess of the hunt, c. 1840s.
Lower center: Beige cameo depicting three-dimensional portrait of Flora, goddess of flowers, c.1840s.
Lower right: Beige cameo depicting portrait of cherub with damage to left side of cameo, c.1840s.
Bottom left: Small gray cameo depicting ram with some damage to right side of cameo, c.1840s.
Bottom center right: Small beige cameo with portrait in profile depicting Apollo with Laurel wreath; there is damage to the left and right sides of the cameo, c.1840s.
Bottom right: Small gray cameo depicting portrait of cherub, c.1840s.

Small cameos are $195-225 each and large cameos are $350-400 each.

Cameo depicting Ceres (Demeter), goddess of the harvest, with wheat and scythe, with some damage to the bottom right of cameo, c. 1840s. $300-350.

An alternative view of (Ceres) Demeter to show relief work in carving.

Cameo depicting angel,
c.1840s. $250-275.

Cameo depicting Artemis (Diana), goddess of
the hunt, with bow, c.1840s. $125-150.

39

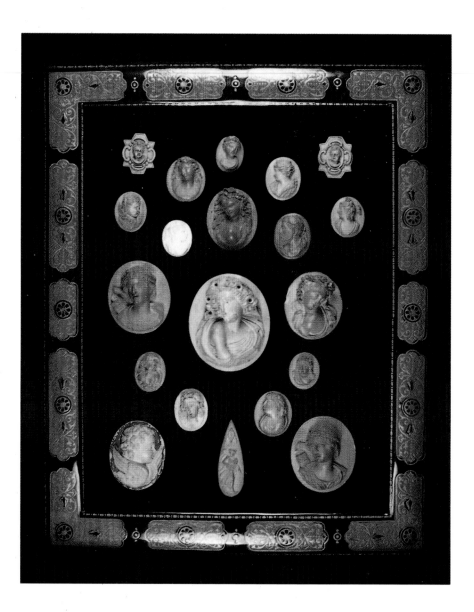

40

Opposite page:

Top left and right: Small gray cameos depicting portraits of cherubs, c.1840s.

Top center left: Beige cameo depicting portrait of Bacchante maiden, follower of Dionysus (Bacchus), god of wine and fertility, with grapes and grape leaves in hair, c.1840s.

Top center: Beige cameo depicting three-dimensional portrait of Roman figure, c.1840s.

Top center right: Beige cameo depicting portrait in profile of angel, c.1840s.

Top left: Beige cameo depicting portrait in profile of cherub, c.1840s.

Top center left: White cameo depicting portrait in profile of Roman man, c.1840s.

Top center: Large Beige cameo depicting three-dimensional portrait of Bacchante maiden, follower of Dionysus (Bacchus), god of wine and fertility, with grapes and grape leaves in hair, c.1840s.

Top center right: Beige cameo depicting portrait in profile of bearded man, c.1850s.

Top center right: Small beige cameo depicting portrait in profile of woman, c.1840s.

Center left: Beige cameo depicting three-dimensional portrait of Artemis (Diana), goddess of the hunt, with crescent moon in hair, c.1840s.

Center: Large beige cameo depicting three-dimensional portrait of woman, c.1840s.

Center right: Beige cameo depicting three-dimensional portrait of Bacchante maiden, follower of Bacchus, god of wine and fertility, with grapes and grape leaves in hair, c.1840s.

Lower left: Small beige cameo depicting cherub, c.1840s.

Lower center left: Small gray cameo depicting portrait of Bacchante maiden, follower of Dionysus (Bacchus), god of wine and fertility with grapes and grape leaves in hair, c.1840s.

Lower center right: Beige cameo depicting portrait in profile of woman, c.1850s.

Lower right: Small beige cameo depicting woman's portrait, c.1840s.

Bottom left: Cameo depicting portrait in profile of cherub, c.1840s.

Bottom center: Beige cameo depicting portrait of muse, c.1840s.

Bottom right: Beige portrait depicting three-dimensional portrait of Artemis (Diana), goddess of the hunt, c.1840s.

Small cameos are $195-225 each and large cameos are $350-400 each.

This profile view shows relief of carving.

Gray cameo depicting Hera, wife of Zeus, wearing a diadem and earrings. There's damage to the nose, ca. 1840s. $150-175.

41

Top left: Brown cameo depicting angel, c.1840s.

Top right: White cameo depicting figure of cherub, c.1850s.

Upper left and right: Two small gray cameos depicting floral motif, c.1840s.

Upper center: Gray cameo depicting Dionysus (Bacchus), god of wine and fertility, with grapes and grape leaves in hair, c.1840s.

Lower left: Large gray cameo depicting portrait in profile of Psyche, bride of Cupid, with butterfly wing in hair, c.1840s.

Lower right: Brown cameo depicting three-dimensional portrait of Bacchante maiden, follower of Dionysus (Bacchus), with grape leaves in hair, c.1840s.

Bottom left: White cameo depicting portrait of figure, c.1840s.

Bottom center: Black cameo depicting portrait of figure, c.1840s.

Bottom right: Small gray cameo depicting portrait in profile of Dionysus (Bacchus), god of wine and fertility, with grapes and grape leaves in hair, c.1840s.

Small cameos are $195-225 each and large cameos are $350-400 each.

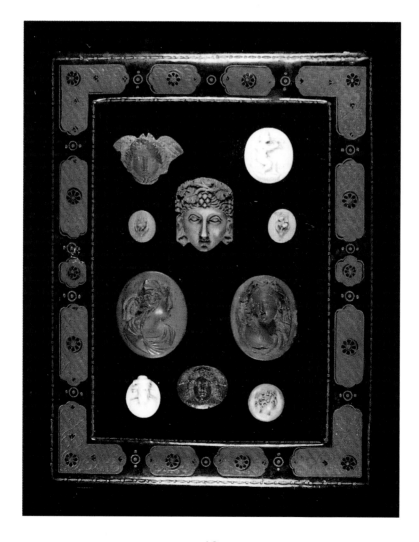

Cameo depicting Athena, goddess of war, c.1840s. $150-175.

Another view of Athena to show relief and detail of carving.

43

Cameo depicting Bacchante maiden, follower of Dionysus (Bacchus), god of wine and fertility, with grape leaves in hair, c.1840s. $175-195.

Beige cameo depicting portrait in profile of man, c.1840s. $200-225.

Beige cameo depicting Hera, wife of Zeus, c.1840s. $275-295.

Another view of Hera to show relief of carving.

Beige cameo depicting Bacchante maiden, follower
of Dionysus (Bacchus), god of wine and fertility, with
grapes and grape leaves in hair (with damage to nose),
c.1840s. $200-300 as is.

Alternate view of Bacchante maiden to
show relief in carving.

Top left: Beige cameo depicting profile of cherub with damage to the right side of cameo, c.1840s.
Top center left: Small beige cameo depicting woman's portrait in profile, c.1840s.
Top center: White cameo depicting cherub, c.1840s.
Top center right: Gray cameo depicting three-dimensional portrait of woman, c.1840s.
Top right: Cameo depicting three-dimensional portrait of cherub in profile, c.1840s.
Upper left: Small cameo depicting portrait of woman in profile with flowers in hair, c.1840s.
Upper center: Cameo depicting cherub, c.1840s.
Upper right: Small beige cameo depicting portrait of cherub, c.1840s.
Center left: Three-dimensional portrait of Artemis (Diana), goddess of the hunt, with some damage to the right of cameo, c.1840s.
Lower center: Small cameo depicting portrait of woman in profile, c.1840s.
Center: Large beige cameo depicting three-dimensional portrait of Bacchante maiden, follower of Dionysus (Bacchus), god of wine and fertility, with grapes and grape leaves in hair, c.1840s.
Lower center: Small beige cameo depicting portrait of bearded man in profile, c.1840s.
Center right: Black cameo depicting portrait of religious figure, c.1840s.
Lower left: Cameo depicting portrait in profile of cherub, c.1840s.
Lower center: Beige cameo depicting three-dimensional portrait of woman, c.1840s.
Lower right: Beige cameo depicting portrait in profile of cherub, c.1840s.

Small cameos are $195-225 each and large cameos are $350-400 each.

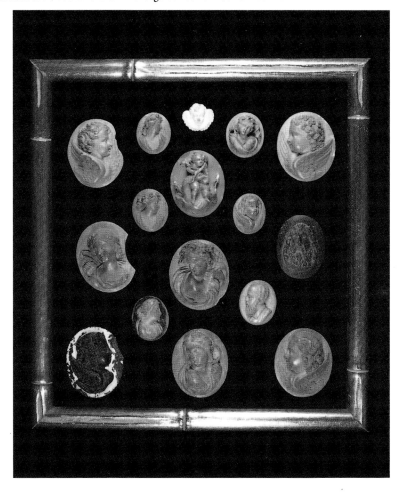

47

Top left: Cameo depicting portrait in profile of bearded man, c.1840s.
Top center: White cameo depicting cherub, c.1840s.
Top right: Beige cameo depicting three-dimensional portrait of muse, c.1840s.
Center left: Small black cameo depicting figure of Cupid, god of love, c.1840s.
Upper center left: Portrait of Roman warrior Heracles, c.1850s.
Center: Large cameo depicting Flora, goddess of flowers, c.1840s.
Upper center right: Cameo depicting portrait in profile of cherub, c.1840s.
Upper center right: Small black cameo depicting cherub, c.1840s.
Center right: Black cameo depicting cherub, c.1840s.
Lower left: White cameo depicting portrait of Caeser, c.1840s.
Lower center left: White cameo depicting portrait in profile of bearded man, c.1840s.
Lower center: Cameo depicting three-dimensional portrait of Bacchante maiden, follower of Dionysus (Bacchus), god of wine and fertility, with grapes and grape leaves in hair, c.1840s.
Lower center right: Large cameo depicting portrait of Bacchante maiden, follower of Dionysus (Bacchus), god of wine and fertility, with grapes and grape leaves in hair, c.1840s.
Lower right: Cameo depicting portrait in profile of cherub, c.1840s.

Small cameos are $195-225 each and large cameos are $350-400 each.

Stone

Book Chain with onyx stones, prong set onyx cameo depicting Psyche, bride of Cupid, and three prong set onyx cameos depicting woman's portrait, c.1890s. $1500-2000.
Courtesy of Teresa J. Rogers.

Right three photos:
Top: Enlarged view of 14KG ring with stone cameo depicting woman's portrait, c.1860s. $2000-2500.
Center: Enlarged view of 14K rose gold sardonyx ring with cameo depicting woman with curls, c.1850s. $2500-3000.
Bottom: 14K rose gold ring with dark stone cameo depicting woman, c.1870s. $2000-2500.

Rings courtesy of Teresa J. Rogers.

1/120 12KG bracelet with filigree work and shell cameos depicting woman's portrait, c.1920s. $1500-2000. *Courtesy of Sue Rainey Pruitt.*

Stickpin with stone cameo depicting religious figure, c.1860s. $800-1200. *Courtesy of Pat Henry, Yesterday's Rose.*

Stone cameo ring depicting woman set in gold, c.1890s. $800-1200. *Courtesy of Mary Liles.*

Left: Fob with twisted gold frame and stone intaglio depicting Ares, god of war, c.1850s. $500-600.
Top center: Loose stone cameo depicting Demeter (Ceres) with stalk of wheat, c.1850s. $300-400.
Bottom center: Fob with twisted gold frame and stone cameo depicting Roman warrior Heracles, c.1850s. $600-700.
Right: Loose fob stone intaglio depicting Ares, god of war, c.1850s. $200-300.

Stone fobs and cameo courtesy of Pat Henry, Yesterday's Rose.

White stone cameo depicting woman set against glass background in brass frame, c.1920s. $200-250.
Courtesy of Ruby Henderson.

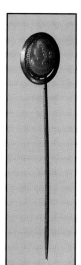

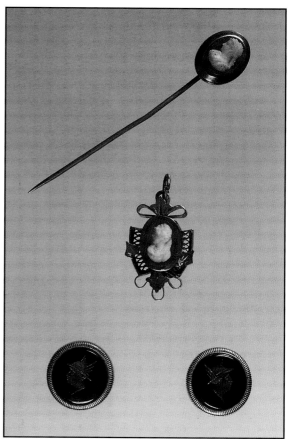

Left: Gold metal stickpin with glass cameo depicting woman, c.1930s. $175-195.
Below center: Gold metal stickpin with onyx cameo depicting woman, c.1890s. $200-225.
Below right: Gold metal stickpin with stone cameo depicting Hera, wife of Zeus, c.1890s. $195-225.

Stickpins courtesy of Melissa Elrod.

Top: Stickpin with stone cameo depicting woman set in gold frame, c.1880s. $200-250.
Center: Gold pendant with leaf motif and filigree work with stone cameo depicting woman, c.1870s. $300-400.
Bottom: Pair of stone intaglios depicting Hermes (Mercury), messenger of the gods, set in gold metal frames, c.1930s. $400-450 for the pair.

Cameos and intaglios courtesy of Jackie McDonald.

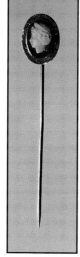

Cameo ring, c. 1890. $425-550. *Courtesy of Will Walker.*

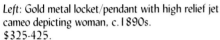

Left: Gold metal locket/pendant with high relief jet cameo depicting woman, c.1890s. $325-425.

Right: Stickpin with jet cameo depicting Athena, goddess of wars, c.1890s. $195-225.

Stickpin and locket courtesy of Jackie McDonald.

Top left: Loose stone cameo depicting woman's portrait, c.1890s. $195-225.
Top right: Loose stone cameo depicting Flora, goddess of flowers, c.1890s. $195-225.
Bottom: Brooch with stone cameo depicting woman's portrait, set in twisted gold metal frame, c.1890s. $350-375.

Stone cameos courtesy of Mary Liles.

Center left: Gutta-percha cameo brooch; depicts muse with birds, c.1890s. $225-325.
Bottom left: Jet cameo depicting Psyche with butterfly wing in hair, set in gold metal frame on brooch with pearls and glass stones, c.1930s.

Brooches courtesy of Great Finds and Designs, Texarkana, Texas.

Brass locket/pendant with prong set stone cameo brooch depicting Psyche, bride of Cupid, set in brass with floral motif, 2" x 1.5", c.1890s. $375-395. *Courtesy of Clarice J. Doback.*

Top: Locket with black enameling and stone cameo; depicts Roman figure, c.1890s. $325-350.
Center right: Heart locket with heart shaped stone cameo depicting woman's portrait, c.1940s. $195-225.
Bottom: Pendant with stone cameo depicting woman's portrait, c.1960s. $195-225.

Cameos courtesy of Roland Hill.

Back of locket/pendant.

Stone cameo ring, c. 1890. $375-450.
Courtesy of Pat Henry, Yesterday's Rose.

Top: Brooch with obsidian cameo depicting woman's portrait set in gold metal frame, c.1950s. $125-150.
Top left: Brooch with obsidian cameo depicting woman's portrait set in silver metal frame, c.1940s. $175-195.
Top right: Brooch with obsidian cameo set in gold metal frame, c.1950s. $225-250.
Center: Brooch with obsidian cameo depicting woman's portrait set in gold metal frame with simulated pearls, c.1940s. $325-350.
Lower left and right: Gold metal earrings with obsidian cameos depicting woman's portrait surrounded by seed pearls, c.1940s. $295-325.

Cameos courtesy of Mary Liles.

Hematite intaglio depicting Hermes (Mercury), messenger of the gods, set in 14K gold setting of ring, c. 1890s. $250-350.
Courtesy of Donna Harp Head.

Hematite intaglio depicting woman's portrait, set in silver metal frame, c.1960s. $195-225.
Courtesy of Yankee.
Courtesy of Ruby Vallie.

Shell

Shell with carving depicting woman and floral motif, c.1890s. $900-1200. *Courtesy of Melissa Elrod.*

Shell cameo brooch/pendant depicting Artemis (Diana), goddess of the hunt, with crescent moon in hair, set in 14KG frame with filigree, c.1860s. $1500-1800. *Courtesy of Jackie McDonald.*

Left: Shell cameo brooch depicting Flora, goddess of flowers, c. 1890. $425-460. *Top:* Shell cameo brooch, depicting Ceres (Demeter), goddess of harvest, c. 1820. $395-425. *Right:* Shell cameo brooch depicting Ceres (Demeter), goddess of harvest, c. 1850. $400-550. *Cameos courtesy of Garden Gate Antiques.*

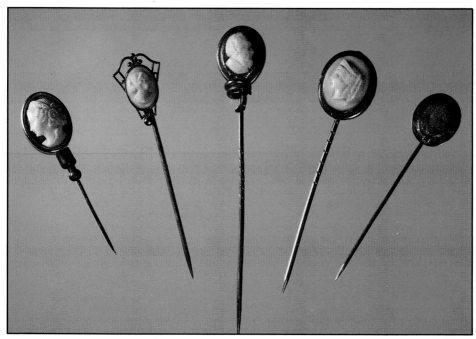

Left: Stickpin with shell cameo depicting woman, c.1890s. $425-475.
Center left: Stickpin with shell cameo depicting woman, c.1880s. $200-300.
Center: Stickpin with shell cameo depicting man, c.1890s. $450-500.
Center right: Stickpin with shell cameo depicting woman, c.1890s. $400-500.
Right: Stickpin with coral cameo depicting woman, c.1890s. $250-350.

Stickpins courtesy of Melissa Elrod.

Left: Loose mother-of-pearl cameo depicting woman wearing wreath of leaves, c.1890. $250-300.
Below: Loose mother-of-pearl cameo depicting Garden of Eden religious scene. $400-500.

Mother-of-pearl cameos courtesy of Melissa Elrod.

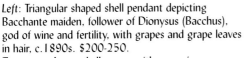

Left: Triangular shaped shell pendant depicting Bacchante maiden, follower of Dionysus (Bacchus), god of wine and fertility, with grapes and grape leaves in hair, c.1890s. $200-250.

Top center: Loose shell cameo with mourning scene, c.1890s. $400-500.

Bottom right: Pendant with prong set shell cameo depicting woman; Phillipe Cotier "Anitmagnetic Swiss Made" watch on reverse, c.1940s. $295-350.

Cameos courtesy of Melissa Elrod.

Top: Pendant necklace with shell cameo depicting Artemis (Diana) with crescent moon in hair set in gold frame with twisted rope effect with seed pearls, c.1880s. $300-400.

Center: Stickpin with prong set coral cameo habillé depicting woman with flowers in hair and metal flower in hair, c.1890s. $350-450.

Bottom: Pendant necklace with prong set cameo, set in gold metal frame, c.1920s. $400-500.

Pendant necklaces and stickpin courtesy of Great Finds and Designs.

Top left: Mother-of-pearl cameo brooch; depicts woman set in gold metal frame with simulated seed pearls and twisted rope effect, c.1940s. $175-195.

Top right: Mother-of-pearl cameo brooch; depicts woman with flowers in hair, set in gold metal frame, c.1950s. $195-225.

Center left and right: Mother-of-pearl cameo earrings depicting woman with curls in hair, c.1940s. $45-55.

Center: Pendant necklace with mother-of-pearl cameo depicting woman, set in elaborate gold metal frame, c.1970s. $150-175.

Mother-of-pearl brooches, earrings, and pendant necklace courtesy of Great Finds and Designs.

Mother-of-pearl cameo depicting woman with short curls, set in Sterling silver frame, c.1930s. $150-175.

Florenza locket/pendant necklace with cameo depicting woman set in gold metal frame, c.1950s. $150-250. Courtesy of Nell Palmer Orr.

Left: Shell cameo brooch depicting woman set in gold metal frame, c.1940s. $195-225.
RightL Shell cameo depicting woman set in gold metal frame with floral motif, c.1880s. $195-225.

Cameos courtesy of Great Finds and Designs.

Shell cameo brooch with scene of Aphrodite with goat, set in twisted gold frame, c.1860s. $1800-2000. *Courtesy of Madonna Waller.*

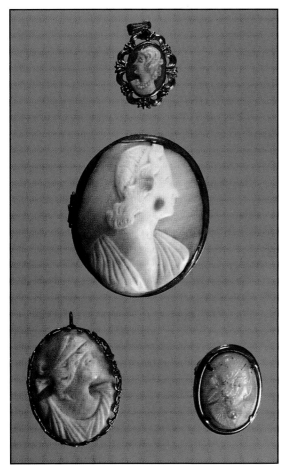

Top: Plastic cameo pendant depicting woman set in gold metal frame, c.1950s. $200-250.
Center: Shell cameo brooch depicting woman, c.1870s. $295-325.
Lower left: Shell cameo pendant depicting Roman woman, c.1880s. $250-350.
Lower right: Prong set glass cameo habillé with seed pearl depicting Roman woman, c.1920s. $125-150.

Cameos courtesy of
Great Finds and Designs.

Shell cameo depicting Flora, goddess of flowers, set in gold metal frame, c.1890s. $900-1200.

Top left: Pendant brooch with shell cameo; depicts woman set in 12K 1-20GF frame with floral motif, c.1930s. $400-500.

Top right: Brooch with prong set shell cameo depicting Roman woman set in gold frame, c.1880s. $400-500.

Bottom left: Button with stone cameo depicting Roman figure set in twisted gold metal frame, c.1890s. $150-175.

Center: Brooch/pendant with shell cameo depicting woman with flowers set in gold frame, c.1920s. $300-400.

Bottom right: Brooch pendant with shell cameo depicting Roman woman glued onto paste background, set in gold twisted frame, c.1890s. $300-400.

Cameos courtesy of Garden Gate Antiques.

Shell cameo brooch depicting Flora, goddess of flowers, set in 12K 1-20GF frame, c.1930s. $1800-2000. *Courtesy of Jean Williams, Garden Gate Antiques.*

Left: Brooch with shell cameo depicting Psyche, bride of Cupid, with butterfly wing in hair set in gold frame with filigree and floral motif, c.1880s. $425-535.

Below: Gold metal bar pin with prong set shell cameo depicting woman, c.1850s. $300-400.

Brooch and bar pin courtesy of Mary Jo Stetzer.

14K gold ring with cameo depicting Roman woman with flowers in hair, c.1870s. $525-625. Courtesy of Donna Hanner.

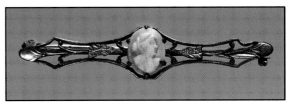

Five loose shell cameos depicting woman's portrait, c.1860s-1880s. $50-75 each. Courtesy of Garden Gate Antiques.

Brooch with shell cameo depicting Ceres (Demeter), goddess of harvest, set in gold frame with filigree, c.1880s. $400-500. Courtesy of Mary Howe.

Mother-of-pearl cameo depicting woman, set in gold metal frame, c.1930s. $95-125. Courtesy of Kenneth L. Surratt, Jr.

61

Top left and right: Sorrento mother-of-pearl earrings, set in Sterling silver, c.1960s. $40-50.
Center: Sorrento mother-of-pearl pendant necklace depicting woman with short hair, set in Sterling silver, c.1970s. $65-95.
Bottom left: Mother-of-pearl pendant depicting woman, c.1890s. $95-125.
Bottom right: Mother-of-pearl brooch with cameo depicting woman set in gold metal frame, c.1920s. $125-150.

Mother-of-pearl cameo jewelry courtesy of Chaney Raley.

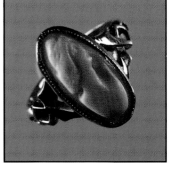

Gold ring with shell cameo depicting woman, set in gold frame, c.1880s. $300-400. Courtesy of Jessie Houston.

Mother-of-pearl brooch depicting woman with long curls, set in silver metal frame, c.1920s. $195-225. Courtesy of Mary Perkins.

Silver ring with coral cameo depicting Bacchante maiden, follower of Dionysus (Bacchus), god of wine and fertility, c.1890s. $250-350. Courtesy of Ruby Henderson.

Top left two photos:
Top: Gold metal bar pin with stone cameo depicting woman set in gold metal frame with seed pearls, c.1880s. $300-400.
Bottom: Shell cameo brooch depicting Artemis (Diana), goddess of the hunt, with crescent moon in hair, set in gold frame with twisted rope effect, c.1860s. $400-500.

Bar pin and brooch courtesy of River City Mercantile Cos., Jefferson, Texas.

Below three photos:
Left: Brooch with shell cameo depicting woman with long curls set in 1/20 12KG GF frame twisted for rope effect, c.1890s. $300-400. Courtesy of Jaci C. Oxner.
Center: Brooch with shell cameo depicting portrait of woman with flowers set in 1/20 12KG GF frame with floral and butterfly motifs, c.1890s. $400-450. Courtesy of Joyce Calhoun..
Right: Pendant with shell cameo depicting woman with short curls and flower on shoulder set in 10K gold frame with floral motif, c.1920s. $300-400.
Courtesy of Chaney Raley.

Gold metal necklace with filigree and three shell cameos depicting woman's portrait, c.1930s. $395-425.
Courtesy of Chaney Raley.

Top: Ring with shell cameo depicting woman set in gold metal frame with four coral stones, c.1920s. $350-400.
Center left: Florenza brooch with shell cameo depicting woman's portrait set in gold metal frame with simulated pearls, c.1960s. $250-300.
Center right: Brooch/pendant with shell cameo; depicts woman with curls set in 800 gold frame, c.1940s. $300-400.
Bottom: Brooch with shell cameo; high relief portrait of woman set in 1/20 12K GF twisted frame, c.1950s. $300-400.

Cameos courtesy of Chaney Raley.

Gold metal bracelet with plastic "stones," rhinestones, and simulated pearls and one plastic cameo depicting portrait of woman. $65-75. *Courtesy of Beverly Jean Yarberry McDowell.*

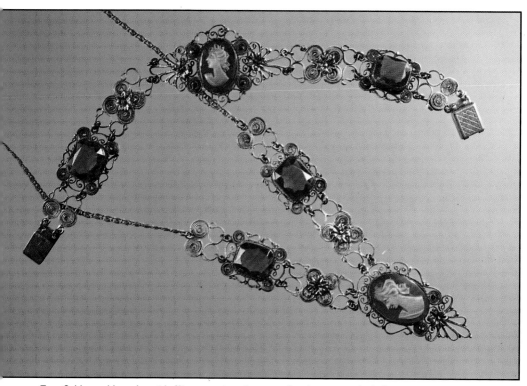

Top: Gold metal bracelet with filigree work and topaz colored stones with shell cameo depicting woman's portrait, c.1940s. $200-300.
Bottom: Necklace with filigree work and topaz colored stones with shell cameo depicting woman's portrait, c.1940s. $350-450.

Shell cameo earrings and pendant necklace set, c.1930s. $325-350. *Courtesy of Jean Elizabeth McDowell Tullis.*

Opposite page, bottom:
Left: Prong set shell cameo ring depicting woman's portrait, c.1930s. $300-400.
Center: Pendant necklace with shell cameo depicting woman's portrait set in gold frame, c.1930s. $250-350.
Right: Shell cameo ring depicting woman with flowers on shoulder set in twisted metal frame, c.1940s. $200-300.

Cameo rings and pendant necklace courtesy of Jean Elizabeth McDowell Tullis.

Mother-of-pearl brooch with two figures, c.1930s. $175-195.
Courtesy of Mary Collom Fore.

Top. Brooch/pendant with shell cameo depicting woman with flowers set in metal frame, c.1890s. $200-300.
Bottom. Brooch and cameo earrings set with prong set shell cameos; depicts woman's portrait, c.1930s. $350-400.

Brooch/pendant and brooch and earrings set courtesy of Shirley Ledbetter Jones.

Left: Loose shell cameo depicting Demeter (Ceres), goddess of the harvest, with wheat in hair, c.1890s. $195-225.
Right: Brooch with shell cameo depicting Flora, goddess of flowers, set in gold frame, c.1920s. $400-500.

Cameos courtesy of Mary Collom Fore.

Left: Shell cameo brooch/pendant depicting portrait of Psyche, bride of Cupid, with butterfly wing on shoulder, set in gold frame, c.1850s. $800-900.

Top center. Shell cameo brooch depicting woman with flowers in hair and on shoulder, set in gold frame with floral motif, c.1890s. $300-400.

Right. Shell brooch/pendant depicting portrait of Psyche, bride of Cupid, with butterfly on shoulder, c.1820s. $900-1200.

Cameos courtesy of Teresa J. Rogers.

Gold bracelet with floral motif and shell cameo depicting woman, c.1890s. $900-1200. *Courtesy of Harriet Autrey.*

Shell with carving, c. 1940. $600-800. *Courtesy of Buddy Rose.*

Shell clip-on earrings and brooch set depicting woman's portrait, set in gold metal frames, c.1950s. $400-500. *Courtesy of Teresa J. Rogers.*

Shell pendant, clip-on earrings, and brooch set depicting woman's portrait, set in gold filled frames, c.1950s. $900-1200. *Courtesy of Teresa J. Rogers.*

Top: Shell cameo depicting Hera, wife of Zeus, wearing diadem, c. 1890. $1500-1800.
Bottom left: Shell cameo depicting Athena, goddess of war, c. 1890. $395-450.
Bottom right: Shell cameo depicting Ceres (Demeter), goddess of Harvest, c. 1880. $650-950.

Opposite page, bottom:
Top left: Brooch with shell cameo depicting Ceres (Demeter), goddess of Harvest, set in gold frame, c.1890s. $400-500. *Courtesy of Helen Floyd.*
Top right: Brooch/necklace with shell cameo depicting woman's portrait, set in gold metal frame, c.1890s. $300-400. *Courtesy of Patsy Alexander.*
Center left: Brooch with gold filigree and seed pearls and shell cameo depicting Apollo with lyre, c.1890s. $900-1200. *Courtesy of Mary B. Jumper.*
Center left and right: Gold clip-on earrings with shell cameos depicting woman's portrait, c.1940s. $250-350. *Courtesy of Patsy Alexander.*
Center: Brooch with shell cameo depicting Flora, goddess of flowers, set in gold filigree frame, c.1930s. $600-800. *Courtesy of Mary Bransford.*
Center right: Brooch with shell cameo depicting Flora, goddess of flowers, c.1860s. $900-1200. *Courtesy of Voncile Martin.*
Bottom: Black velvet bracelet with shell cameo depicting Roman figure set in gold frame with twisted gold, c.1860s. $900-1200. *Courtesy of Patsy Alexander.*

Left: Brooch with shell cameo depicting Artemis (Diana), goddess of the hunt, with crescent moon in hair, set in gold frame. $400-500. *Top center*. Brooch with shell cameo; depicts woman's portrait set in gold frame with filigree, c.1940s. $300-400. *Right*: Brooch with shell cameo depicting woman's portrait, set in elaborate gold metal frame, c.1930s. $400-500.

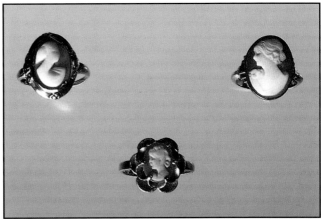

Top left: 10KG ring with shell cameo depicting woman's portrait, c.1940s. $250-275. *Lower center*: Gold ring with prong set shell cameo depicting woman with curls in hair, c.1940s. $225-250. *Top right*: Gold ring with shell cameo; depicts woman with flower in hair, c.1930s. $275-295.

Cameo rings courtesy of Mary Liles.

Brooch with shell cameo depicting woman's portrait, set in 1/20 12KG frame, c.1950s. $200-300. *Courtesy of Nell Palmer Orr.*

Left: Shell cameo brooch, c. 1890. $350-425. *Top*: Shell cameo brooch, c. 1920. $250-300. *Bottom*: Shell cameo pendant, c. 1890. $325-415. *Right*: Shell cameo, c. 1990. $295-350. *Cameos courtesy of pat Henry, Yesterday's Rose.*

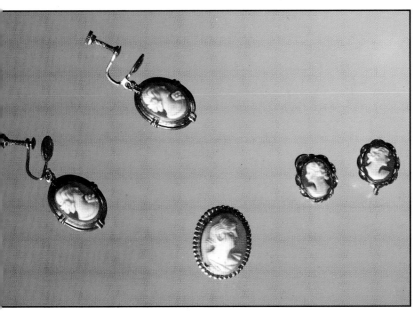

Left: Screw back earrings with cameos depicting woman with flower on shoulder, set in gold metal frames, c.1940s. $195-225. *Center*: Brooch with shell cameo depicting woman's portrait, set in gold metal frame, c.1950s. $95-125. *Right*: Screw back earrings with shell cameos depicting woman with curls, set in twisted gold frames, c.1950s. $125-150.

Earrings and brooch courtesy of Mary Liles.

Top left and right: Pierced earrings with shell cameos depicting woman's portrait, set in twisted gold metal frames, c.1960s. $75-95.

Top center: Earrings with shell cameos depicting woman's portrait, set in gold metal filigree frames, c.1950s. $125-150.

Center left and right: Pierced earrings with shell cameos depicting woman with flowing hairstyle (part of earring on right is missing), c.1960s. $55-65 as is.

Bottom center: Clip-on earrings with shell cameos depicting woman's portrait, set in gold metal frames, c.1940s. $125-150.

Cameo earrings courtesy of Mary Liles.

Left: Brooch/pendant with mother-of-pearl cameo depicting woman, set in gold metal frame, c.1950s. $125-150.
Right: Pendant with mother-of-pearl cameo depicting woman, set in silver metal filigree frame, c.1960s. $95-125.

Mother-of-pearl cameos courtesy of Mary Liles.

Top right: Plastic cameo pendant, c. 1960. $65-95.
Right: Plastic cameo pendant, c. 1980. $35-65.

Cameos courtesy of Garden Gate Antiques.

Top left: Shell cameo pendant depicting woman's portrait, set in Sterling silver filigree flower shaped frame, c.1920s. $150-175.
Top right: Shell pendant with prong set cameo depicting woman's portrait, set in Sterling silver frame, c.1920s. $175-195.
Center: Shell cameo pendant depicting woman with curls, set in Sterling silver frame with beading, c.1980s. $225-250.
Lower left: Shell pendant depicting woman with short curls, set in Sterling silver frame, c.1940s. $275-295.
Lower right. Brooch/ pendant depicting woman with flowers in hair and on shoulder, set in Sterling silver frame, c.1980s. $295-325.

Cameos courtesy of Teresa J. Rogers.

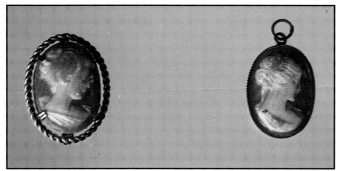

Left: Brooch with prong set shell cameo depicting woman's portrait, set in twisted metal frame, c.1890s. $325-350.
Right: Pendant with shell cameo depicting woman's portrait, set in gold metal frame, c.1890s. $295-325.

Brooch and pendant courtesy of Mary Liles.

Top left: Bracelet with shell cameo depicting woman's portrait set in gold metal frame with filigree and seed pearls with damage to right side of bracelet, 1923. $150-200.
Top center: Brooch with shell cameo; depicts woman's portrait set in gold frame, c.1890s. $125-150.
Top right: Round brooch with shell cameo depicting woman's portrait, set in gold frame, c.1890s. $125-150.
Center left: Gold pendant with rhinestone drop and prong set shell cameo depicting woman's portrait, c.1890s. $195-225.
Center: Gold cross with shell cameo depicting woman's portrait, c.1950s. $195-225.
Center right: Gold pendant with leaf motif and prong set shell cameo depicting woman's portrait, set in twisted gold frame, c.1920s. $275-295.
Bottom left: Watch with shell cameo depicting woman's portrait (watch is on reverse side), c.1940s. $195-225.
Bottom right: Silver pendant with prong set shell cameo depicting woman with flower on shoulder, c.1930s. $195-225.

Cameo jewelry courtesy of Mary Liles.

Top: Brooch with prong set cameo; depicts woman, with flower on shoulder, set in brass frame, c.1890s. $300-400.

Center left: Brooch with shell cameo depicting woman's portrait, set in brass frame with beads, c.1890s. $300-400.

Center right: Florenza brooch with prong set shell cameo depicting woman's portrait surrounded by seed pearls in gold metal frame, c.1950s. $200-300.

Bottom: Brooch with shell cameo; depicts woman with curls set in gold metal frame with floral motif, c.1890s. $300-400.

Cameo brooches courtesy of Mary Liles.

Near right: Brooch with shell cameo depicting woman with flowers on shoulder set in gold metal frame, c.1890s. $250-350.
Far upper right: Gold metal ring with shell cameo depicting woman's portrait, c.1890s. $195-225.
Far lower right: Gold metal filigree ring with shell cameo depicting woman's portrait, c.1920s. $225-250.

Brooch and rings courtesy of Sarah Jones.

Top: Pendant necklace with shell cameo depicting Demeter (Ceres), goddess of the harvest, with stalk of wheat set in gold frame, c.1890s. $400-500.
Center left: Brooch with shell cameo depicting woman's portrait, set in gold frame with floral motif, c.1930s. $200-300.
Center right: Brooch with shell cameo depicting woman's portrait, set in gold frame (damage to left side of frame), c.1890s. $150-200.
Bottom center: Brooch with shell cameo depicting woman with curls, set in twisted gold frame, c.1890s. $300-400.

Cameo jewelry courtesy of Mary Liles.

Florenza brooch/pendant with shell cameo depicting woman's portrait set in gold metal frame with simulated pearls, c.1950s. $200-300. Courtesy of Carolyn Payne.

Shell brooch/pendant set depicting portrait of woman, c.1920s. $300-400.
Courtesy of Frances Hubbard.

Top: Brooch/pendant with shell cameo; depicts woman with flowers, set in gold frame, c.1920s. $350-450.

Center left: Brooch/pendant with shell cameo depicting Bacchante maiden, follower of Dionysus (Bacchante), set in gold metal frame, c.1890s. $200-300.

Lower center: Loose cameo with portrait of Roman woman with curls with damage to the upper right of cameo, c.1890s. $95-125.

Center right: Brooch with shell cameo depicting woman's portrait, set in twisted gold frame. $200-300.

Lower left: Brooch/pendant with shell cameo depicting woman with flowers, set in gold filigree frame, c.1890s. $200-300.

Lower right: Pendant with shell cameo; depicts woman with flowers in hair, set in gold frame with floral motif, c.1920s. $260-360.

Cameo jewelry courtesy of Mary Liles.

Shell cameo clip-on earrings and brooch/pendant necklace set with 19-inch chain depicting woman's portrait, c.1890s. $395-425. *Courtesy of Frances Hubbard.*

Dixelle pendant with shell cameo depicting woman with curls set in gold frame, c.1960s. $165-225. *Courtesy of Darlene Dixon.*

Top: Shell cameo pendant, c. 1920. $350-475.
Bottom: Shell cameo necklace, c. 1920. $500-650.

Cameos courtesy of Garden Gate Antiques.

Left: Brooch with shell cameo depicting woman's portrait, set in gold metal frame with leaf motif and gold metal beads, c.1950s. $200-300.
Center: Brooch with shell cameo depicting woman's portrait, set in gold metal frame with simulated pearls, c.1950s. $250-350.
Right: Brooch with prong set shell cameo depicting woman's portrait, set in gold frame with twisted metal and leaf motif, c.1950s. $200-300.

Cameo brooches courtesy of Great Finds and Designs.

Top: Brooch with shell cameo, set in gold metal frame with simulated pearls and faux turquoise beads, c.1950s. $200-300.

Center left: Brooch with prong set shell cameo depicting woman's portrait surrounded by simulated pearls, set in gold metal frame, c.1950s. $200-300.

Center right: Pendant with shell cameo depicting woman's portrait, set in gold metal frame, c.1890s. $300-400.

Bottom: Brooch with shell cameo depicting woman's portrait, set in gold metal frame, c.1920s. $300-400.

Cameos courtesy of Great Finds and Designs.

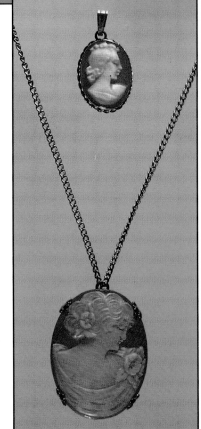

Top: Enlarged view of shell pendant, set in gold frame, 0.5" x 0.625", c.1940s. $200-300.
Bottom: Enlarged view of pendant necklace with prong set cameo depicting woman adorned with flowers, 1.25" x 0.88", c.1930s. $300-400.

Cameos courtesy of Martha Watkins.

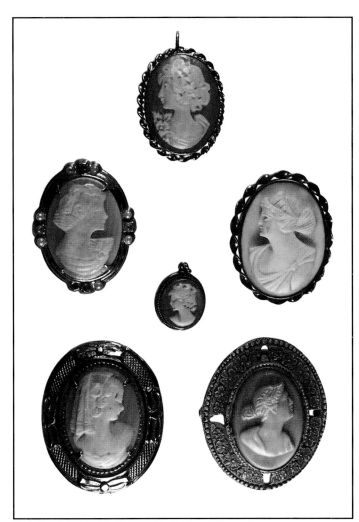

Top: Pendant with shell cameo depicting woman with wreath of flowers in hair, set in gold frame, c.1920s. $300-400.

Center left: Brooch with shell cameo depicting woman with roses in hair, set in gold metal frame with rhinestones and simulated pearls, c.1940s. $400-500.

Center: Pendant with shell cameo depicting woman's portrait, set in gold metal frame, c.1950s. $150-250.

Center right: Pendant with shell cameo depicting woman's portrait, set in gold metal twisted frame, c.1890s. $300-400.

Lower left: Brooch with prong set shell cameo depicting woman with long curls, set in gold metal frame, c.1920s. $300-400.

Lower right: Brooch with shell cameo depicting woman's portrait, set in gold metal frame, c.1890s. $350-450.

Cameo jewelry courtesy of Great Finds and Designs.

Above: Shell clip-on earrings depicting woman's portrait, set in silver frames, c.1950s. $150-200.
Right: Shell cameo brooch depicting figure of woman and bearded man, set in gold metal frame, c.1980s. $350-400.

Cameos courtesy of Chaney Raley.

Left: Shell brooch with woman's portrait, set in 1/20 10KG frame with leaf motif, c.1890s. $300-400.

Top center: Shell brooch/pendant with woman adorned with flowers, set in 12KG frame with floral motif, c.1920s. $500-600.

Right: Shell brooch/pendant with woman's portrait, set in gold frame, c.1890s. $250-350.

Cameos courtesy of Nancy Rainey Granich.

Left: Shell brooch depicting woman adorned with flowers in hair and on shoulder, set in gold frame with floral motif, c.1880s. $300-400.

Center: Cameo habillé pendant depicting woman adorned with flowers in hair and on shoulder, set in gold metal frame, c.1920s. $300-400.

Right: Shell brooch depicting woman adorned with flowers, set in gold frame, c.1890s. $300-400.

Cameos courtesy of Bernice Ney Johnson.

Shell pendant depicting woman's portrait, set in 925 Sterling silver frame, c.1960s. $200-300. *Courtesy of Memory Lane Mall.*

Top: Shell brooch depicting woman adorned with flowers in hair and on shoulder, set in gold frame, c.1930s. $200-300.
Bottom: Bar pin with plastic cameo depicting woman, set in gold metal frame, c.1960s. $45-55.

Cameos courtesy of Kathy Wommack.

Top: Shell brooch depicting woman's portrait, set in gold metal frame with beads, c.1890s. $900-1200.
Bottom: Coro shell brooch with portrait of woman with flower on shoulder, set in gold metal frame with floral motif, c.1950s. $150-200.

Cameos courtesy of Ruby Vallie.

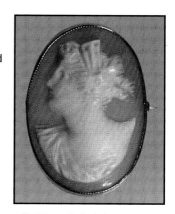

Shell brooch depicting Psyche, bride of Cupid, with butterfly wing in hair, set in gold frame, c.1890s. $300-400. *Courtesy of Ruby Vallie.*

Top: Florenza brooch with shell cameo depicting portrait of woman, surrounded by simulated seed pearls set in gold metal frame with fleur-de-lis motif, c.1960s. *Courtesy of Kenneth L. Surratt, Jr.* $200-300.

Center left: Cameo pendant depicting woman's portrait, set in gold metal frame, c.1890s. *Courtesy of Jackie McDonald.* $150-250.

Center right: Shell pendant; depicts Dionysus (Bacchus), god of wine and fertility, with grape leaves in hair, set in gold frame, c.1880s. $325-425.

Bottom: Rectangular brooch depicting Rebecca at the Well motif, set in twisted gold metal frame, c.1860s. $1200-1500.

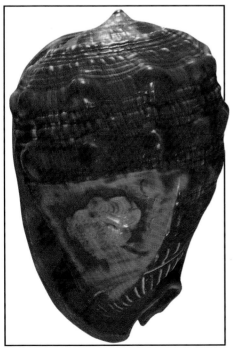

Shell with carved portrait of woman, 5" x 3.5", c.1990s. $800-900.
Courtesy of Donna Harp Head.

Left: Loose shell cameo depicting woman's portrait, c.1990s. $85-105.
Top center: Small loose cameo depicting woman with flower in hair, c.1990s. $70-85.
Right: Loose shell cameo depicting woman with flower in hair, c.1990s. $85-105.

Cameos courtesy of Donna Harp Head.

Krementz earrings, with portrait of woman, set in gold filled frames, c.1990s. $135-160.
Courtesy of Ray Harp Jewelers.

Van Dell shell pendant depicting portrait of woman, set in 14KG frame, c.1990s. $350-400.
Courtesy of Ray Harp Jewelers.

Van Dell shell pendant with woman's portrait, set in gold filled 14KG frame, c.1990s. $200-250.
Courtesy of Ray Harp Jewelers.

Top left: Loose shell cameo depicting woman's portrait, c.1990s. $95-125.
Top right: Loose shell cameo depicting woman with upswept hair, c.1990s. $75-95.
Center: Small shell cameo depicting woman's portrait, c.1990s. $45-55.
Lower left: Brooch/pendant with shell cameo depicting woman, set in gold frame, c.1990s. $225-325.
Courtesy of Donna Harp Head.
Lower center: Two loose shell cameos depicting woman's portrait, c.1990s. $45-55 each.
Lower right: Heart shaped brooch/pendant depicting woman with curls, set in 14KG frame, c.1990s.
$275-295.

Unless otherwise noted, the cameos are courtesy of Ray Harp Jewelers.

Van Dell white on blue cameo pendant depicting cat, set in 14KG frame, c.1990s. $325-375. Courtesy of Ray Harp Jewelers.

Van Dell lever back earrings with shell cameos depicting woman's portrait, set in gold frames, c.1990s. $125-150. Courtesy of Ray Harp Jewelers.

Shell brooch/pendant; depicts woman, set in 14KG frame, 1" x 1.25", c.1990s. $265-295.
Courtesy of John Head.

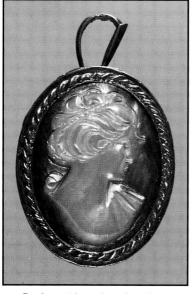

Pendant with mother-of-pearl cameo depicting woman, set in silver frame, c.1930s. $195-225. Courtesy of Donna Harp Head.

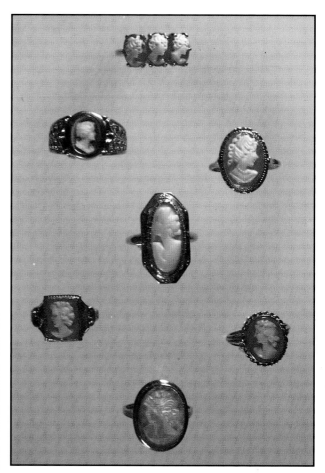

Top: Gold metal ring with three prong set shell cameos depicting women, c.1950s. $175-195.
Top left: 14KG Van Dell ring with white on blue shell cameo depicting woman, c.1990s. $465-495. Courtesy of Ray Harp Jewelers.
Top right: Gold metal ring with shell cameo depicting woman's portrait, c.1950s. 200-225.
Center: Gold metal ring with shell cameo depicting woman, c.1930s. $225-250. Courtesy of Suzanne Goodson Hutt.
Lower left: 14KG Van Dell ring with shell cameo depicting woman, c.1990s. $350-400. Courtesy of Ray Harp Jewelers.
Lower right: Gold metal ring with shell cameo depicting woman with curls in hair, c.1960s. $175-195.
Bottom: Gold metal ring with mother-of-pearl cameo depicting woman, c.1980s. 150-175.

Unless otherwise noted, the rings are courtesy of Donna Harp Head.

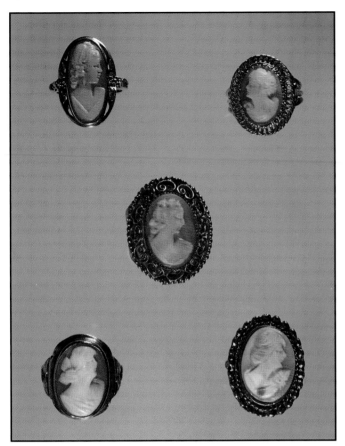

Top left: Sterling silver ring with shell cameo depicting woman with flower in hair, c.1960s. $175-195.
Top right: 14KG ring with shell cameo depicting woman with short curls, c.1930s. $225-250.
Center: Gold filled filigree ring with shell cameo depicting woman's portrait, c.1940s. $250-275.
Lower left: 10KG ring with shell cameo depicting woman with flower in hair, c.1920s. $250-275.
Lower right: Gold ring with cameo depicting woman with flower on shoulder, c.1940s. $175-195.

Rings courtesy of Teresa J. Rogers.

Mother-of-pearl cameo pendant depicting portrait of woman, set in silver frame, c.1960s. $95-125.
Courtesy of Chaney Raley.

Top Left: Brooch with mother-of-pearl cameo depicting woman with flower surrounded by marcasites and two garnets, set in silver frame, c.1980s. $95-125.
Top Right: Brooch with mother-of-pearl cameo depicting woman with upswept hair surrounded by onyx and marcasites, set in silver frame, c.1980s. $175-195.

Mother-of-pearl cameos courtesy of Teresa J. Rogers.

Wallet with attached mother-of-pearl cameo depicting woman's portrait set against abalone background, c.1930s. $125-150. *Courtesy of Teresa J. Rogers.*

Above:

Left: Shell pendant with cameo depicting woman with curls, set in gold filled frame, c.1950s. $225-325.

Top left: Prong set shell cameo depicting woman's portrait, set in gold frame, c.1890s. $300-400.

Center: Shell pendant with cameo depicting woman with flowers in hair and on shoulder, set in gold filled frame, c.1940s. $430-580.

Top right: Small prong set cameo pendant depicting woman with flowers in hair and on shoulder, set in gold filled frame, c.1920s. $210-315.

Right: Heart shaped cameo pendant depicting woman with flowers in hair and on shoulder, set in gold filled frame, c.1930s. $300-400.

Cameos courtesy of Teresa J. Rogers.

Left:

Top: Mother-of-pearl prong set pendant depicting Roman warrior, set in gold frame, c.1890s. $125-150.

Bottom: Shell brooch/pendant depicting woman with flower on shoulder, set in gold frame, c.1942. $300-400.

Cameos courtesy of Virginia Payne Hargrove.

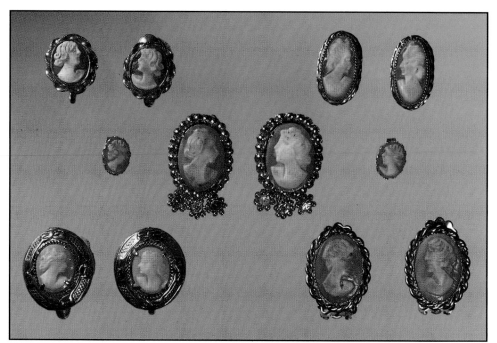

Top left: Shell clip-on earrings depicting woman, set in gold metal frames, c.1920s. $150-200.
Top right: Shell earrings depicting woman, set in gold frames, c.1930s. $175-195.
Center left and right: Shell earrings depicting woman, set in gold frames, c.1940s. $95-125.
Center: Coro shell earrings depicting Psyche, bride of Cupid, with butterfly wing in hair, set in gold metal beaded frames with three rhinestones at bottom of earrings, c.1950s. $225-250.
Bottom left: Shell prong set clip-on earrings, set in gold metal frame with floral motif, c.1940s. $175-195.
Bottom right: Shell clip-on earrings depicting woman, set in gold metal frames. $125-150.

Earrings courtesy of Mary Perkins.

Top left: Shell cameo brooch depicting woman with curls, set in gold frame with leaf motif, c.1930s. 200-300.

Top center: Shell cameo brooch depicting woman with flowers in hair, set in gold frame with filigree, c.1890s. $250-350.

Top right: Shell cameo brooch depicting woman with flowers in hair and on shoulder, set in gold frame with leaf motif, c.1890s. $200-300.

Bottom: Gold metal mesh bracelet with floral motif glass stones and prong set shell cameo depicting woman, c.1940s. $175-195.

Cameos courtesy of Mary Perkins.

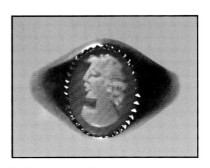

Gold metal ring with shell cameo depicting woman's portrait, c.1950s. $225-250. *Courtesy of Roland Hill.*

Opposite page, bottom:

Top left: Shell cameo brooch depicting woman with flowers in hair and on shoulder, set in gold metal frame, c.1930s. $300-400.

Center: Loose shell cameo depicting woman with upswept hair, c.1950s. $95-125.

Top right. Shell cameo brooch depicting woman with flowers, set in gold metal frame, c.1890s. $415-520.

Bottom: Gold metal bracelet with four shell cameos depicting various portraits of women, c.1940s. $200-300.

Cameos courtesy of Mary Perkins.

Top left: Shell cameo pendant depicting woman with flower in hair, set in twisted gold frame, c.1930s. $200-300.

Top right: Shell cameo pendant depicting woman with upswept curls, set in gold metal frame, c.1940s. $195-225.

Center: Gold metal link bracelet with two shell cameos; depicts woman with flowers in hair and on shoulder, c.1940s. $225-250.

Bottom left: Shell cameo pendant; depicts woman adorned with flowers in hair and on shoulder, set in gold metal frame, c.1890s. $300-400.

Bottom right: Shell cameo brooch depicting woman with flowers in hair and on shoulder, set in gold metal frame, c.1920s. $350-450.

Cameos courtesy of Mary Perkins.

Left: Shell cameo pendant depicting woman, set in 14KG filigree frame, c.1860s. $400-500.
Right: Shell cameo pendant depicting Psyche, bride of Cupid, set in gold frame, c.1880s. $300-400.

Cameos courtesy of Kenneth L. Surratt, Jr.

Top left: Loose shell cameo depicting woman wearing wreath of flowers (damage to shell), c.1860s. $95-125 as is. Center: Prong set shell cameo brooch depicting woman's portrait, set in gold metal frame, c.1890s. 200-300. Top right: Shell cameo brooch depicting Dionysus (Bacchus), god of wine and fertility, with grape leaves in hair, set in gold metal frame, c.1880s. $300-400.
Shell cameos courtesy of Mary Perkins.

Enlarged view of signed shell cameo brooch depicting three-dimensional portrait of woman, 1965. $500-600. Courtesy of Helen Morice.

Top: Shell cameo brooch, c. 1980. $295-325. Center: Shell cameo pendant, c. 1840. $250-300. Bottom left: Shell cameo brooch, c. 1820. $325-395. Bottom right: Shell cameo brooch, c. 1820. $450-500.
Cameos courtesy of Garden Gate Antiques.

Above: Bone cameo pendant with silver frame, c. 1970. $95-125.
Right: Mother-of-pearl pendant, c. 1930. $75-95.

Pendants courtesy of Pat Henry, Yesterday's Rose

Gold cuff bracelet with shell cameo depicting woman with flower in hair, c. 1920s. $800-900.
Courtesy of Roland Hill.

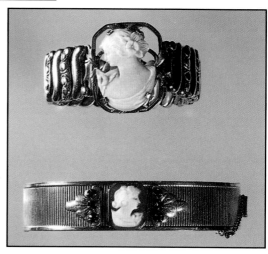

Right top: Gold filled bracelet with prong set shell cameo depicting woman with flowers in hair and on shoulder, c. 1920s. $700-900.
Right bottom: Gold filled bracelet with shell cameo depicting woman with flowers in hair and on shoulder and garnet stones on each side, c. 1920s. $400-500.
Bracelets courtesy of Teresa J. Rogers.

Gold filled bracelet with shell cameo depicting woman's portrait, c. 1920s. $1500-2000.
Courtesy of Teresa J. Rogers.

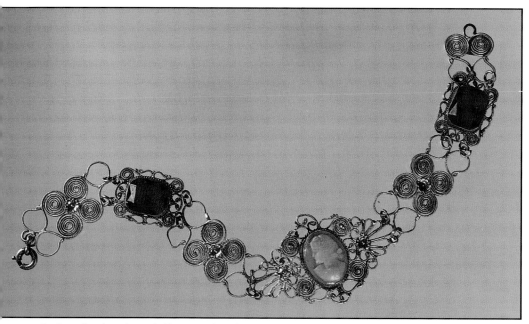

Sterling silver bracelet with filigree work, red stones, and shell cameo depicting woman's portrait, c.1920s. $1800-2200. *Courtesy of Teresa J. Rogers.*

Top: Shell cameo brooch, c. 1960. $225-300.
Center: Shell cameo brooch, c. 1880. $250-300.
Bottom: Shell cameo locket, c. 1920. $225-295.

Cameos courtesy of Garden Gate Antiques.

Top: 10KG ring with prong set cameo depicting Dionysus (Bacchus), god of wine and fertility, c.1940s. $195-225. *Center:* 14KG ring with cameo depicting woman with upswept hair, c.1920s. $310-345. *Lower left:* 14KG ring with cameo depicting woman's portrait, c.1870s. $225-250. *Lower right:* 14KG ring with cameo depicting Psyche, bride of Cupid, with butterfly wing in hair, c.1870s. $195-225. *Rings courtesy of Teresa J. Rogers.*

Left: Shell cameo brooch/pendant depicting woman with jewelry and flowers, set in Sterling silver frame, c.1980s. $400-500. *Right*: Shell cameo brooch/pendant depicting woman adorned with flowers, set in Sterling silver frame, c.1980s. $315-440.

Cameos courtesy of Teresa J. Rogers.

Top: Gold bracelet with six prong set shell cameos depicting woman's portrait, c.1970s. $250-275. *Bottom*: Gold filled bracelet with shell cameo depicting Psyche, bride of Cupid, with butterfly wing in hair, c.1940s. $900-1200.

Bracelets courtesy of Teresa J. Rogers.

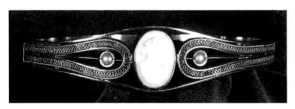

Gold bracelet with filigree, seed pearls, and stone cameo depicting woman, c.1880s. $1500-2000. Courtesy of River City Mercantile Co.

Top left: Gold metal locket with shell cameo depicting portrait of woman, c.1940s. $195-225.

Top right: Shell cameo depicting woman with short curls, c.1920s. $225-250.

Center: Brooch with plastic cameo depicting woman's portrait, set in gold metal frame with simulated pearl, c.1950s. $45-55.

Bottom left: Brooch with prong set cameo depicting woman's portrait surrounded by seed pearls, set in gold frame, c.1890s. $200-300.

Bottom right: Brooch with prong set cameo depicting woman's portrait, set in gold frame with floral motif, c.1890s. $200-300.

Cameos courtesy of Teresa J. Rogers.

14KG ring with shell cameo, depicting woman's portrait, c.1890s. $200-300.
Courtesy of Penny Smith.

Left. Shell cameo depicting woman's portrait, set in 14KG frame, c.1980s. $200-300.
Courtesy of Janis E. Clements.
Right. Shell cameo depicting muse with lyre, c.1980s. $400-500.
Courtesy of Frances Swann More.

Necklace with shell cameo
depicting woman's portrait
surrounded by yellow gold filled
frame, c. 1950s. $200-300.
Courtesy of Janet Stark.

Brooch with three shell cameos depicting women's portraits, all set
in yellow gold-filled twisted frames, c. 1980s. $350-400. *Courtesy
of Donna Harp Head.*

Shell cameo depicting Flora,
goddess of flowers, set in
twisted gold frame, c. 1990s.
$200-300. *Courtesy of Donna
Harp Head.*

Shell brooch; depicts woman's
portrait set in 14K gold frame
with beading, c. 1990s.
$350-400. *Courtesy of Donna
Harp Head.*

Shell cameo brooch/pendant
depicting Hera, wife of Zeus,
wearing diadem, set in yellow
gold-filled engraved frame with
Etruscan beading. It has some
damage to cameo, c. 1890s.
$300-350. *Courtesy of Donna
Harp Head.*

Shell brooch cameo depicting
Psyche, bride of Cupid, with
butterfly on shoulder, set in gold
frame, c. 1960s. $250-300.
Courtesy of Donna Harp Head.

Shell cameo brooch/pendant
depicting woman with flower on
shoulders, set in twisted gold
frame, c. 1990s. $250-300.
Courtesy of Donna Harp Head.

Shell cameo depicting portrait of
woman set in 18K gold ring,
ca. 1930s. $250-275. *Courtesy
of Donna Harp Head.*

Bracelet with six shell cameos depicting woman's portrait set in gold, c. 1960s. $350-450. *Courtesy of Donna Harp Head.*

Bracelet with eight shell cameos depicting woman's portrait set in sterling silver, c. 1950s. $400-500. *Courtesy of Donna Harp Head.*

Steling silver ring with mother-of-pearl cameo depicting woman, c.1960s. $75-95. *Courtesy of Carol Gordon.*

Top: Gold metal brooch with prong set cameo depicting woman with curls, c.1920s. $200-300.
Center left: Pendant with shell cameo depicting Psyche, bride of Cupid, with butterfly on shoulder, set in gold frame with leaf motif, c.1890s. $400-500.
Center right: Brooch with prong set cameo depicting Hebe feeding the eagle (Zeus), set in twisted gold frame, c.1890s. $425-545.
Bottom: Brooch with cameo depicting woman with flowers in hair, c.1890s. $200-300.

Brooch with shell cameo depicting woman's portrait, set in silver filigree frame. *Courtesy of Carol Paton.* $300-400.

Loose mother-of-pearl cameo depicting woman, c.1930s. $75-95. *Courtesy of Mary Collom Fore.*

Glass

Art earrings and bracelet with cameos depicting woman's portrait surrounded by seed pearls and rhinestones, c.1950s. $450-500. *Courtesy of Mary Liles.*

Left: Glass cameo necklace, c. 1960. $65-95.
Right: Glass cameo necklace, c. 1960. $70-105.
Cameos *courtesy of Iris Bohanan.*

Brooch with prong set glass cameo depicting woman with flowers in hair, set in brass frame, c.1920s. $85-105. *Courtesy of Great Finds and Designs.*

Top: Sarah Coventry "Shadow Cameo" glass ring depicting portrait of woman with flower on shoulder, c.1950s. $35-45.
Bottom: Intaglio ring depicting flower, top flips over to reveal turquoise cabochon. $55-65.

Top: Brooch with glass intaglio depicting Roman soldier, set in gold metal frame, c.1960s. $45-55.
Center left: Earring with intaglio depicting woman's portrait, set in gold metal frame (one earring missing), c.1960s. $40-50 for the pair.
Center right: Earring with plastic cameo with woman's portrait, set in gold frame (one earring missing), c.1960s. $40-50 for the pair.
Center: Earring with intaglio, set in gold metal twisted frame (one earring missing), c.1960s. $35-45 for the pair.
Lower left and right: Glass intaglio earrings depicting woman's portrait, set in gold metal twisted frames, c.1920s. $45-55.

Brooch and earrings courtesy of Mary Liles.

Top left: White on green prong set glass cameo depicting woman, set in gold metal frame, c.1950s. $45-55.
Top right: Prong set glass cameo depicting woman, c.1890s. $50-60.
Bottom left: Black glass cameo depicting woman, c.1960s. $45-55.
Bottom center: Black glass intaglio, set in gold metal frame, c.1960s. $35-45.
Bottom right: White on pink glass cameo depicting woman with some damage to cameo, c.1950s. $35-45.

Cameos courtesy of Kathy McCoy.

Whiting & Davis gold metal filigree bracelet with reverse intaglio glass cameo depicting woman's portrait, c.1950s. $55-70.
Courtesy of Teresa J. Rogers.

Above:
Left: Pendant with glass cameo depicting woman set in gold metal frame with four plastic "stones," c.1960s. $40-50.
Right: Pendant with glass cameo set in gold metal frame. $55-65.

Cameos courtesy of Mary Liles.

Gold metal necklace with glass intaglio fob, depicting woman's portrait and locket. $55-65.
Courtesy of Mary Liles.

Sarah Coventry gold
metal necklace with
glass intaglio depicting
woman, c.1960s.
$45-55.
Courtesy of Mary Liles.

46-inch silver metal belt with glass intaglio
depicting woman's portrait. $65-75.
Courtesy of Mary Liles.

Left: Sarah Coventry glass intaglio depicting woman's portrait set in gold metal frame, c.1960s. $25-35.
Center: Pendant necklace with black glass intaglio depicting woman's portrait, c.1960s. $45-55.
Right: Pendant with glass cameo set in silver metal frame. $35-45.

Cameo and intaglios courtesy of Kenneth L. Surratt, Jr.

Silver metal bracelet with glass cameo depicting woman's portrait, c.1960s. $65-75.
Courtesy of Marianne Mason.

Left:
Top: Brooch with pink glass cameo depicting woman, set in gold metal frame, c.1940s. $65-75.
Bottom: Brooch with glass intaglio depicting woman, set in frame with simulated pearls and plastic "stones," c.1960s. $55-65.

Cameo and intaglio courtesy of Mary G. Moon.

Top: Earrings with glass cameos depicting woman's portrait, set in gold metal frames, c.1970s. $35-45.
Center left: Coral colored glass cameo depicting woman with flowers in hair and on shoulder, set in gold metal frame with leaf motif, c.1950s. $55-65.
Center right: Tortoiseshell colored glass cameo depicting woman's portrait, set in gold metal frame, c.1970s. $45-55.
Bottom: Florenza clip-on earrings with prong set blue glass cameos depicting woman's portrait, set in gold metal frames, c.1950s. $45-55.

Cameos courtesy of
Teresa J. Rogers.

22-inch silver metal necklace with glass cameo depicting woman set in gold metal frame. $65-75.
Courtesy of Mary Liles.

105

Top: Green glass intaglio earrings; depicts woman's portrait set in gold metal frames, c.1950s. $55-65.

Center left and right: Mother-of-pearl cameo earrings depicting Roman soldier, set in metal frames, c.1940s. $55-65.

Bottom: Green glass cameo earrings, set in gold metal frames, c.1960s. $65-75.

Intaglios and cameos courtesy of Mary Liles.

Prong set glass intaglio clip-on earrings depicting woman, set in gold frames. $55-65.
Courtesy of Memory Lane Mall.

Black glass on white cameo depicting woman's portrait set in gold metal frame with simulated pearls, c.1960s. $55-65.
Courtesy of Kenneth L. Surratt, Jr.

Ring with glass intaglio portrait in gold frame with pearls, c. 1950. $95-150.
Courtesy of Iris Bohanan.

West Germany style pendant with glass cameo; depicts woman set in gold metal frame with four glass stones, c.1970s. $95-125. *Courtesy of Chaney Raley.*

Top: Brooch with glass cameo depicting woman, set in gold metal frame with colored glass stones and rhinestones, c.1950s. $65-75.
Left: Brooch with black on white cameo depicting Psyche, bride of Cupid, with butterfly wing in hair, set in twisted gold metal frame, c.1950s. $75-85.
Center: Pendant with glass cameo depicting warrior, c.1970s. $35-45.
Right: Brooch/pendant with white on black glass cameo depicting woman set in silver metal frame, c.1960s. $55-65.

Cameos courtesy of Great Finds and Designs.

White on pink earrings and brooch set depicting woman with flower on shoulder, set in gold metal frames, c.1990s. $50-65. Courtesy of Janis E. Clements.

West German set with necklace and earrings depicting a portrait of woman set with pearls and stones on gold frame, c. 1960. $295-325.
Courtesy of Donna Head.

Clip-on earrings and brooch set with glass cameos depicting woman surrounded by colored glass stones, c.1960s. $98-135. *Courtesy of Great Finds and Designs.*

Left: Brooch with jet cameo depicting Psyche, bride of Cupid, with butterfly wing in hair, set in gold metal frame, c.1940s. $75-95.
Center: Brooch with glass cameo depicting woman with flowers in hair, set in twisted gold metal frame, some damage to left side of cameo, c.1960s. $65-75.
Right: Brooch with glass cameo depicting Psyche, bride of Cupid, with butterfly wing in hair, set in gold metal frame (some damage to cameo), c.1940s. $55-65 as is.
Cameos courtesy of Chaney Raley.

Galette gold metal necklace with locket and glass intaglio depicting woman, c.1960s. $65-75. *Courtesy of Memory Lane Mall.*

Above: Reverse glass intaglio depicting two birds on branch, c.1950s. $25-35. *Right*: Glass cameo depicting woman's portrait, c.1950s. $35-45.

Intaglio and cameo courtesy of Mary Liles.

West Germany set depicting woman's portrait with glass pendant, set in metal with simulated pearls and glass stones, and clip-on earrings, set in gold metal with simulated pearls, c.1960s. $295-325. *Courtesy of Memory Lane Mall.*

Left: Glass intaglio pendant depicting woman, set in gold metal frame with four simulated pearls, c.1960s. $45-55.
Center: Gold metal stickpin with glass intaglio, c.1970s. $20-30.
Right: Glass cameo pendant depicting woman set in gold metal frame, c.1960s. $55-65.

Glass intaglios and cameo courtesy of Ruby Vallie.

Gold metal bracelet and pendant set with glass intaglios depicting woman's portrait. $195-225.
Courtesy of Roland Hill.

112

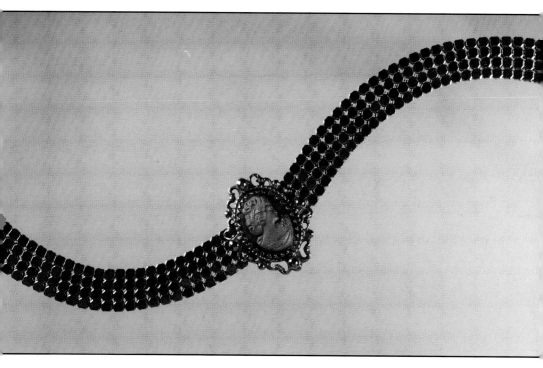

Silver metal choker with glass cameo depicting woman with curls and flower on shoulder, c.1950s. $70-80. *Courtesy of Teresa J. Rogers.*

Glass cameo brooch depicting woman set in gold metal frame, c.1930s. $45-55. *Courtesy of Great Finds and Designs.*

Silver metal ring with glass intaglio depicting woman's portrait, c.1970s. $45-55. *Courtesy of Robin D. Gartee.*

Plastics

Round plastic Japan cameo depicting floral and bird motifs, c.1950s. $55-65. *Courtesy of Melissa Elrod.*

Top left and right: Plastic cameo earrings depicting woman's portrait, set in gold metal frames with simulated pearl drops, c.1950s. $45-55. *Bottom:* Plastic cameo brooch with woman's portrait, set in gold metal twisted frame, c.1950s. $45-55.

Cameos courtesy of Cathy McCoy.

Top left and right: Plastic cameo earrings set in gold metal frames, c.1970s. $35-45.
Center: Pink plastic brooch depicting woman set in gold metal frame, c.1930s. $55-65.
Bottom left and right: Plastic cameo cuff links depicting Psyche, bride of Cupid, with butterfly wing in hair, set in gold metal frames, c.1960s. $45-55.

Earrings, brooch, and cuff links courtesy of Jackie McDonald.

Sarah Coventry brooch with plastic cameo depicting woman with flowers on shoulder set in gold metal frame with faux ruby stones and rhinestones, c.1960s. $45-55. *Courtesy of Mary Liles.*

Pierced earrings and choker set with plastic cameos depicting woman, c.1960s. $55-65.
Courtesy of Mary Liles.

SWANK cuff links with plastic cameos depicting Zeus with one of his lovers set in gold metal, c.1960s.
$58-68. *Courtesy of Charles Terry.*

Brooch with plastic cameo depicting floral motif set in gold metal frame, c.1960s. $45-55.

Plastic cameo brooch, c. 1960. $60-75. *Courtesy of Garden Gate Antiques.*

Plastic cameo brooch signed PERI, c. 1960. $45-55. *Courtesy of Jean Williams.*

Gold metal pendant necklace with plastic cameo depicting Three Muses, c.1960s. $60-70. *Courtesy of Clyda Cox and Augusta Dumas.*

Left: Pendant necklace with white on green plastic PERI cameo depicting woman, set in gold metal frame, c.1960s. $38-48.
Top center: Earrings with plastic cameos depicting woman set in gold metal, c.1960s. $25-35.
Bottom center: Pierced earrings with mother-of-pearl cameos depicting woman set in gold metal frame, c.1960s. $24-35.
Right: Brooch with plastic cameo depicting woman's portrait, c.1960s. $35-45.

Cameo jewelry courtesy of Cora Imogene Hunt Yarberry.

Left. Whiting & Davis brooch with glass cameo depicting woman, set in gold metal frame. $55-65.
Right. Brooch with plastic cameo depicting floral motif, set in gold metal frame. $45-55.

Cameos courtesy of Wanda Goodmon.

Pill box with plastic cameo depicting man and woman. $45-55.
Courtesy of Wanda Goodmon.

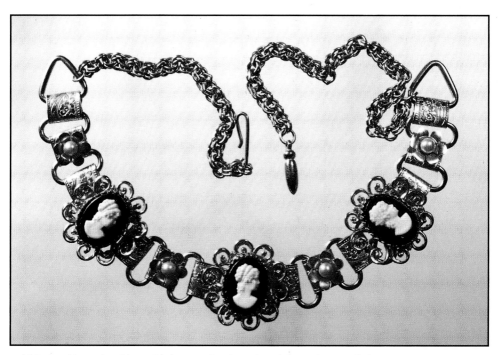

17-inch gold metal necklace with four simulated pearls and three white on black plastic cameos depicting woman, c.1960s. $65-75. *Courtesy of Wanda Goodmon.*

Left: Pendant with plastic cameo depicting woman, set in gold metal frame, c.1960s. $45-55.
Center: Pendant necklace with plastic cameo; depicts woman set in gold metal frame, c.1960s. $45-55.
Right: Pendant with tassel and plastic cameo depicting woman, c.1960s. $45-55.

Cameos courtesy of Mary Liles.

Pair of loose plastic cameos depicting man and woman. $45-50 each.
Courtesy of Mary Liles.

Top: Coro brooch with white on black cameo depicting woman surrounded by rhinestones, set in metal frame with simulated pearls and rhinestones, c.1950s. $65-75.
Center left: Locket/pendant with white on black cameo depicting woman, set in gold metal. $55-65.
Center right: Pendant with plastic cameo habillé depicting woman, set in gold metal frame. $45-55.
Bottom: Brooch with white on black plastic cameo depicting woman with flowers on shoulder, set in silver metal frame, c.1960s. $65-75.

Cameos courtesy of Mary Liles.

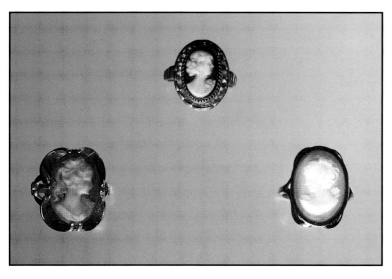

Top: Ring with white on black plastic cameo depicting woman surrounded by rhinestones, set in silver metal, c.1950s. $35-45.
Left: Ring with prong set plastic cameo depicting woman, set in gold metal, c.1970s. $55-65.
Right: Ring with plastic cameo, set in gold metal, c.1970s. $35-45.

Cameo rings courtesy of Mary Liles.

Gold metal wire hoop necklace and pendant with plastic cameo depicting woman, c.1970s. $35-45.
Courtesy of Mary Liles.

Opposite page, bottom:

Top left: Pendant necklace with white on black plastic cameo depicting woman with flowers set in gold metal frame, c.1960s. $45-55.

Top center: Octagonal shaped brooch with plastic cameo; depicts woman with curls, c.1960s. $55-65.

Top right: Brooch with plastic cameo depicting woman with flowers, set in gold metal frame, c.1970s. $25-35.

Center left: Pendant necklace with plastic cameo depicting woman with curls, set in twisted gold metal frame, c.1960s. $25-35.

Center: Brooch with prong set plastic cameo depicting Psyche, bride of Cupid, with butterfly wing in hair, set in gold metal frame with simulated pearls, c.1960s. $55-65.

Lower center left. Pendant with white on black cameo depicting woman with flowers, set in silver metal. $50-60.

Center left: Loose white on black plastic came depicting Psyche, bride of Cupid, with butterfly wing in hair, c.1950s. $15-25.

Center: Loose cameo depicting woman with flowers in hair, c.1960s. $45-55.

Center right: Loose white on blue cameo depicting woman, c.1960s. $20-25.

Lower left: Pendant with plastic cameo depicting woman with flowers on shoulder, set in gold metal, c.1970s. $30-40.

Lower center: Loose cameo depicting cherubs. $30-40.

Lower right: Pendant necklace with plastic cameo depicting woman, set in silver metal with metal drops, c.1960s. $45-55.

Cameos courtesy of Mary Liles.

Left: Loose plastic cameo depicting woman, c.1960s. $20-30.
Center: Large loose plastic cameo depicting woman, c.1960s. $30-40.
Right: Small loose plastic cameo depicting woman, c.1960s. $20-30.

Cameos courtesy of Mary Liles.

Top: Brooch with plastic cameo depicting woman, set in gold metal frame, c.1960s. $50-60.
Center left: Brooch with plastic cameo depicting woman, set in gold metal frame with fleur-de-lis motif, c.1960s. $45-55.
Center right: Brooch with plastic cameo depicting woman, set in gold metal frame, c.1960s. $45-55.
Center: Brooch with plastic cameo depicting woman surrounded by white plastic beads, set in gold metal frame, c.1970s. $70-80.
Lower left: Brooch with plastic cameo depicting woman, set in gold metal frame, c.1960s. $50-60.
Lower right: Brooch with plastic cameo depicting woman surrounded by simulated seed pearls, set in gold metal frame, c.1950s. $50-60.

Cameos courtesy of Mary Liles.

124

Top left: Brooch/pendant with plastic cameo depicting woman with flowers on shoulder, set in gold metal frame, c.1970s. $45-55.
Top right: PERI brooch/pendant with plastic cameo depicting woman, set in gold metal frame, c.1960s. $35-45.
Center: Pendant with plastic cameo depicting two muses, set in gold metal frame; pendant opens to reveal perfume glacé, c.1960s. $65-95.
Lower left: Brooch with prong set plastic white on blue cameo depicting woman, set in gold metal frame, c.1960s. $55-65.
Lower right: Brooch/pendant with white on blue plastic cameo depicting woman, set in metal frame with rhinestones, c.1960s. $55-65.

Cameos courtesy of Mary Liles.

Brooch with plastic cameo depicting woman set in gold metal frame with rhinestones (one is missing), c.1960s. $65-75 as is. *Courtesy of Carol Gordon.*

Opposite page, bottom:
Left: Locket/pendant with plastic cameo depicting woman, set in gold metal frame with floral motif, c.1950s. $45-55.
Right: Brooch with plastic cameo depicting woman, set in gold metal frame. $45-55.

Cameos courtesy of Carol Gordon.

Silver metal and rhinestones bracelet with five prong set plastic cameos depicting woman with flower on shoulder, c.1960s. $125-150. *Courtesy of Teresa J. Rogers.*

Gold metal brooch with simulated pearls and plastic cameo depicting Three Muses, c.1980s. $95-125. *Courtesy of Great Finds and Designs.*

Top: Brooch with black plastic cameo depicting Roman figure, set in gold metal, c.1960s. $55-65. *Center left and right*: Pair of plastic brooches depicting woman, c.1950s. $45-55. *Lower center*: Brooch/ pendant with plastic cameo depicting Psyche, bride of Cupid, with butterfly wing in hair, c.1940s. $105-135.

Cameos courtesy of Great Finds and Designs.

Bottom left: Brooch with white on black plastic cameo depicting woman, set in gold metal frame, c.1960s. $75-85. *Bottom right*: Round brooch with white on black plastic cameo depicting Ceres (Demeter), goddess of the harvest, set in gold metal frame with Etruscan style design, c.1980s. $80-105. *Cameos courtesy of Great Finds and Designs.*

Top: Brooch with plastic cameo habillé depicting woman, set in gold metal frame, c.1950s. $55-65.
Center left: Brooch with plastic cameo depicting woman with flowers in hair, c.1960s. $45-55.
Center right: Brooch with plastic cameo depicting woman, set in gold metal, c.1960s. $65-75.
Lower center: Brooch with plastic cameo depicting woman with flowers in hair and on shoulder surrounded by glass stones, c.1950s. $75-95.

Cameos courtesy of Great Finds and Designs.

Left: Brooch with plastic cameo depicting woman, set in gold metal frame, c.1960s. $45-55.
Right: Brooch/pendant with plastic cameo depicting woman surrounded by simulated pearls, set in gold metal frame, c.1970s. $65-75.

Cameos courtesy of Great Finds and Designs.

Top left: Brooch with glass cameo depicting woman on plastic background, set in gold metal frame, c.1970s. $45-55.

Top right: Heart shaped pendant with white on black plastic cameo depicting woman, set in silver metal frame with rhinestones, c.1950s. $55-65.

Center left: Round brooch with plastic cameo depicting woman with flowers, set in gold metal frame, c.1960s. $55-65.

Center: Brooch with white on black plastic cameo depicting woman, set in white plastic and clear Lucite frame, c.1950s. $65-75.

Center right: Brooch with white on black plastic cameo depicting woman, set in gold metal frame, c.1960s. $65-75.

Bottom: Brooch with prong set white on black plastic cameo depicting woman, set in gold metal frame, c.1970s. $65-75.

Cameos courtesy of Great Finds and Designs.

Top: Brooch with white on green plastic cameo depicting woman set in gold metal frame. $25-35.
Center left: Brooch with prong set plastic cameo depicting woman adorned with flowers set in silver metal twisted frame, c.1960s. $65-75.
Center right: Brooch with white on blue plastic cameo depicting woman set in gold metal frame. $65-75.
Bottom: Brooch with white on black glass cameo depicting woman set in gold metal frame, c.1960s. $75-85.

Cameos courtesy of Great Finds and Designs.

Top: Corocraft floral motif brooch with two white on black plastic cameos; depicts woman and faux topaz stone, c.1960s. $125-150.
Bottom left: Pendant with glass cameo depicting two mythological figures, c.1960s. $75-95.
Bottom right: Brooch with glass cameo depicting woman with gold metal frame, c.1960s. $50-60.

Cameos courtesy of Great Finds and Designs.

Opposite page, bottom:
Top left: Brooch with plastic cameo; depicts woman set in gold metal frame, c.1970s. $45-55.
Bottom center: Brooch with plastic cameo depicting woman set in gold metal frame with rhinestones, c.1960s. $50-60.
Top right: Brooch with plastic cameo depicting woman adorned with flowers set in gold metal frame with floral motif, c.1960s. $65-75.

Cameos courtesy of Great Finds and Designs.

Brooch with white on green plastic cameo depicting woman, set in gold metal frame, c.1970s. $45-55. Courtesy of Mary G. Moon.

Left: Brooch with plastic cameo depicting woman with flowers, set in gold metal frame, c.1960s. $65-75.

Top center: Brooch with plastic cameo depicting woman, set in gold metal frame with simulated pearls, c.1960s. 65-75.

Right: Brooch with plastic cameo depicting woman with curls, set in beaded silver metal frame, c.1970s. $45-55.

Cameos courtesy of Great Finds and Designs.

White on blue plastic brooch/pendant with cameo depicting woman's portrait surrounded by simulated pearls, c.1950s. $65-75. Courtesy of Teresa J. Rogers.

Max Factor Classic Cameo Compact
with plastic cameo depicting woman
with flower on shoulder, opens to reveal
powder, c.1970s. $65-75.
Courtesy of Carolyn Payne.

Another view of the Max Factor Classic Cameo Compact with box.

Top: Brooch with white on blue plastic cameo depicting woman surrounded by rhinestones, colored "stones," and simulated pearls, c.1960s. $50-60.
Center left: Brooch with plastic cameo depicting woman, set in beaded gold metal frame, c.1960s. $45-55.
Center right: Brooch with plastic cameo depicting woman, set in gold metal frame with floral motif, c.1970s. $55-65.
Bottom: Brooch with plastic cameo depicting woman, set in gold metal frame, c.1960s. $75-85.

Cameos courtesy of
Kenneth L. Surratt, Jr.

Left: Brooch with jet cameo depicting woman, c.1890s. $150-175.
Right: Brooch with black plastic cameo depicting Psyche, bride of Cupid set on Lucite, c.1950s. $95-125.

Cameos courtesy of Garden Gate Antiques.

Top left: Pendant with prong set white on black plastic cameo depicting woman, set in gold metal frame, c.1960s. $55-65.
Top right: Brooch with white on black plastic cameo depicting woman with flowers, set in gold metal frame, c.1960s. $55-65.
Bottom: Brooch with white on black plastic cameo depicting woman, set in gold metal frame with five rhinestones. $70-85.

Cameos courtesy of Kenneth L. Surratt, Jr.

Left: Music box/pendant with white on blue plastic cameo depicting woman with roses, c.1970s. $75-85.
Right: Silver metal pill box with white on black plastic cameo depicting woman, c.1960s. $45-55.

Music box and pill box courtesy of Chaney Raley.

135

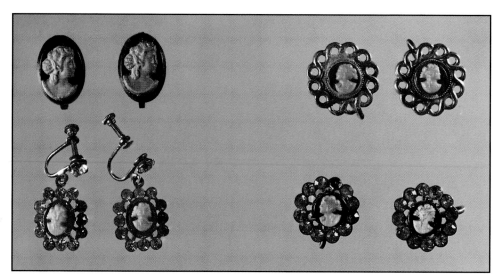

Top left: Screw-on earrings with white on black plastic cameos, c.1950s. $45-55.
Top right: Clip-on earrings with plastic cameos depicting Psyche, bride of Cupid, with butterfly wing in hair, set in gold metal frames, c.1960s. $55-65.
Bottom left: Screw-on earrings with plastic cameos depicting Psyche, bride of Cupid, with butterfly wing in hair surrounded by rhinestones, c.1960s. $75-85.
Bottom right: Clip-on earrings with white on black plastic cameos depicting Psyche, bride of Cupid, with butterfly wing in hair surrounded by rhinestones, c.1950s. $55-65.

Cameo earrings courtesy of Kenneth L. Surratt, Jr.

Left: Locket/pendant necklace with plastic cameo depicting woman, set in gold metal frame, c.1950s. $75-95.

Center: Pendant with plastic cameo depicting woman, set in gold metal frame, c.1970s. $55-65.

Right: Pendant necklace with plastic cameo depicting woman, set in silver metal frame, c.1960s. $55-65.

Cameos courtesy of Kenneth L. Surratt, Jr.

Opposite page, bottom:

Left: Lisner brooch with plastic cameo depicting woman, set in gold metal filigree frame, c.1960s. $67-75.

Top center: Gold metal ring with plastic cameo depicting woman, c.1970s. $45-55.

Bottom center: Earrings with plastic cameos depicting woman set in gold metal frames, c.1970s. $45-55.

Right: Avon locket with plastic cameo depicting woman with flowers, set in gold metal frame, c.1980s. $65-75.

Cameos courtesy of Chaney Raley.

Celluloid brooch cameo depicting woman with roses, c.1920s. $65-75.
Courtesy of Chaney Raley.

Left: Gold metal stickpin with plastic cameo depicting woman, c.1970s. $25-35.
Top center: Brooch with plastic cameo depicting Psyche, bride of Cupid, with butterfly wing in hair, set in gold metal frame with simulated pearls, c.1960s. $55-65.
Center left and right: Clip-on earrings with prong set plastic cameos depicting Psyche, bride of Cupid, with butterfly wing in hair, set in gold metal frames, c.1960s. $35-45.
Bottom center: Pendant necklace with plastic cameo depicting woman, set in gold frame, c.1960s. $45-55.
Right: Brooch with plastic cameo depicting woman, set in gold metal frame, c.1960s. $45-55.

Cameo jewelry courtesy of Chaney Raley.

Left: Brooch with white on black plastic cameo depicting woman, c.1960s. $35-45.
Center: Pendant necklace with white on black plastic cameo depicting woman with upswept hair surrounded by simulated seed pearls, c.1960s. $55-65.
Right: Brooch with white on black plastic cameo depicting woman, c.1960s. $45-55.

Cameos courtesy of Chaney Raley.

Top: Sarah Coventry white on black plastic earrings depicting woman's portrait set in silver metal frames, c.1950s. $50-60.
Center: White on blue earrings depicting woman's portrait set in gold metal frames, c.1960s. $35-45.
Bottom: Screw back earrings with plastic cameos set in gold metal frames with simulated pearls, c.1950s. $55-65.

Earrings courtesy of Ruby Vallie.

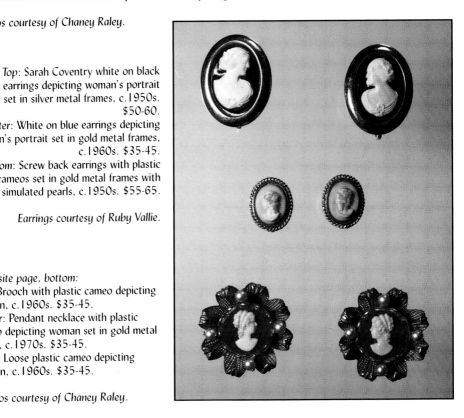

Opposite page, bottom:
Left: Brooch with plastic cameo depicting woman, c.1960s. $35-45.
Center: Pendant necklace with plastic cameo depicting woman set in gold metal frame, c.1970s. $35-45.
Right: Loose plastic cameo depicting woman, c.1960s. $35-45.

Cameos courtesy of Chaney Raley.

Top: White on black plastic brooch, c.1960s. $35-45.
Center left: White on black Avon cameo habillé brooch, set in gold metal, c.1980s. $55-65.
Center right: White on black cameo brooch depicting Psyche, bride of Cupid, with butterfly wing in hair, set in gold metal frame with three rhinestones and four simulated pearls, c.1950s. $75-85.
Bottom center: Brooch with plastic cameo depicting woman's portrait set in gold metal frame with glass stones, c.1950s. $75-85.

Cameos courtesy of Ruby Vallie.

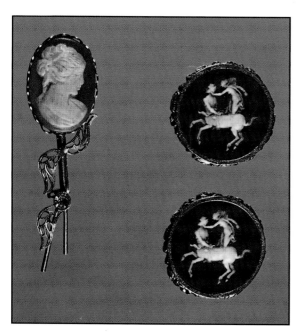

Left: Gold metal brooch with rhinestone and plastic cameo depicting woman's portrait, c.1960s. $45-55.
Right: Pair of plastic cuff-links with scene, set in gold metal frames, c.1970s. $55-65.

Cameos courtesy of Evelyn Kacos.

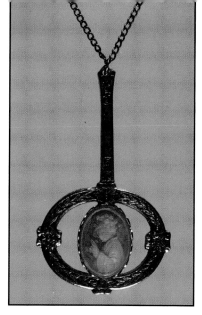

Pendant with plastic cameo depicting woman, set in gold metal key shaped frame, c.1960s. $45-55.
Courtesy of Memory Lane Mall.

Left: Brooch with plastic cameo depicting woman against pink glass background, surrounded by simulated seed pearls, set in gold metal frame, c.1960s. $45-55.
Center: Cameo habillé, with portrait depicting woman, set in gold metal frame, c.1960s. $65-75.
Right: Signed Corday perfume glacé locket, with plastic cameo depicting woman playing lute, set in gold metal frame, c.1970s. $65-75.

Cameos courtesy of Ruby Vallie.

Above:
Top: Giovanni plastic cameo brooch depicting woman, set in gold metal frame, 1960s. $35-45.
Bottom left: Plastic cameo pendant depicting woman, set in gold metal frame, c.1950s. $45-55.
Top center: Plastic cameo earrings depicting woman, set in gold metal frames, c.1960s. $35-45.
Bottom center: Plastic cameo pendant depicting portrait of woman, set in gold metal frame, c.1960s. $35-45.
Bottom right: Avon plastic cameo brooch depicting woman with flower on shoulder, set in gold metal frame, c.1970s. $45-55.
Cameos courtesy of Cathy McCoy.

Below:
Left: Plastic cameo pendant depicting woman with flower on shoulder, set in gold metal frame, c.1980s. $45-55.
Right: Gold metal pill box with white on green plastic cameo depicting woman with flowers on shoulder, c.1960s. $45-55.
Cameos courtesy of Kenneth L. Surratt, Jr.

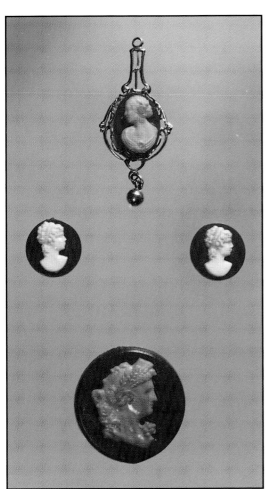

Top: Shell cameo pendant depicting woman with flower in hair, set in gold metal frame with drop, c.1950s. $48-58.
Center: Pair of loose cameos depicting woman's portrait, c.1960s. $35-45.
Bottom: Loose cameo depicting woman, c.1960s. $35-45.

Cameos courtesy of Cathy McCoy.

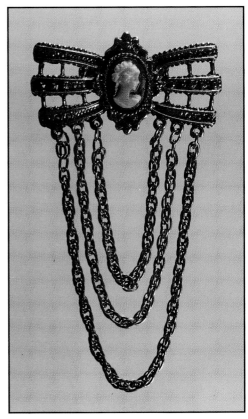

Brooch with white on black plastic cameo; depicts woman, set in silver metal frame, c.1950s. $58-68.
Courtesy of Roland Hill.

Left: Celluloid cameo brooch depicting woman with flower on shoulder, set in gold metal frame with raised design, c.1890s. $95-125.
Center: Sarah Coventry shell cameo brooch; depicts woman set in gold metal frame, c.1970s. $45-55.
Right: Cameo brooch depicting woman, set in gold metal frame, c.1970s. $45-55.

Cameos courtesy of Cathy McCoy.

Top left and right: White on black plastic cameo clip-on earrings depicting woman's portrait, set in gold metal frames, c.1940s. $45-55.

Top center left: Loose white on black plastic cameo depicting Psyche, bride of Cupid, with butterfly wing in hair, c.1950s. $15-25.

Top center right: White on black heart shaped pendant depicting woman's portrait, set in silver metal frame, c.1950s. $35-45.

Center left: White on black plastic cameo brooch depicting woman, set in gold metal frame with floral motif, c.1950s. $45-55.

Center: Loose white on black plastic cameo depicting woman, c.1950s. $45-55.

Center right: White on black cameo pendant depicting Psyche, bride of Cupid, with butterfly wing in hair, set in gold metal frame, c.1940s. $48-58.

Lower left: White on blue prong set pendant depicting woman with flower in hair, c.1950s. $35-45.

Lower center: White on black plastic cameo brooch depicting Psyche, bride of Cupid, with butterfly wing in hair, set in silver metal frame, c.1940s. $55-65.

Lower right: White on blue plastic cameo depicting woman with flowers, set in gold metal frame, c.1960s. $55-65.

Cameos courtesy of Mary Perkins.

Loose plastic cameo depicting woman with flowing hair, c.1960s. $25-35. *Courtesy of Mary Collom Fore.*

Opposite page:
Coro white on blue earrings and brooch set in gold metal frames with rhinestones, c.1950s. $98-128. *Courtesy of Kenneth L. Surratt, Jr.*

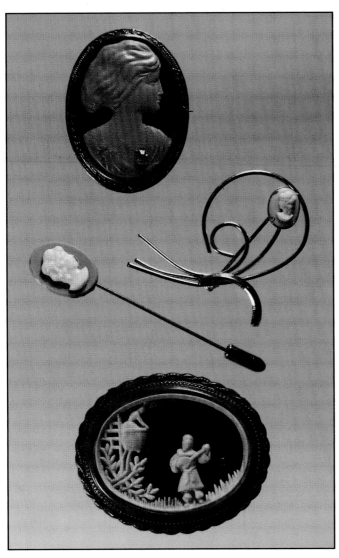

Top: White on black cameo habillé brooch depicting woman with glass stone, set in gold metal frame, c.1890s. $75-95 *Center left*: White on blue stickpin, c.1970s. $15-25. *Center right*: Gold metal brooch with prong set white on blue plastic cameo depicting woman, c.1970s. $15-25. *Bottom*: Celluloid black and white brooch with scene, set in gold metal frame, c.1890s. $55-65. *Courtesy of Helen Morice.*

Unless otherwise noted, the cameo jewelry is courtesy of Roland Hill.

Left: Silver metal ring with celluloid cameo depicting woman with flowers, c.1890s. $75-95. *Right*: Gold metal ring/pillholder with plastic cameo depicting woman's portrait, c.1950s. $65-75.

Rings courtesy of Teresa J. Rogers.

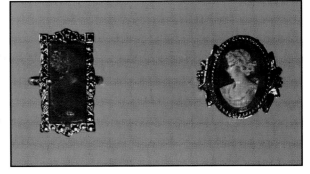

Top left and right: Earrings depicting woman's portrait set in gold metal frames with rhinestones, c.1970s. $55-65.
Bottom center: Pill box with scene of man and woman, c.1970s. $55-65.

Earrings and pill box courtesy of Roland Hill.

Pendant necklace with plastic cameo depicting woman set in gold metal frame with plastic "stones" and 24-inch chain, c.1960s. $48-58.
Courtesy of Mary G. Moon.

147

Pendant with prong set white on black cameo surrounded by aurora borealis stones, c.1960s. $55-65. *Courtesy of Teresa J. Rogers.*

Left: Brooch with plastic cameo depicting woman with flowers, set in gold metal frame with floral motif, c.1960s. $55-65.
Center: Brooch with plastic cameo depicting woman with flowers, set in gold metal frame with simulated pearls, c.1960s. $65-75.
Right: Brooch with plastic cameo depicting woman's portrait, set against redwood background, c.1960s. $55-65.

Cameos courtesy of Teresa J. Rogers.

Top: Clip-on earrings with plastic cameos set in metal frames with glass stones, c.1950s. $45-55.

Center top. Pierced earrings with plastic cameo earrings, c.1960s. $45-55.

Center left and right: Clip-on glass earrings with cameos depicting woman's portrait, c.1960s. $25-35.

Center bottom: Earring with plastic cameo surrounded by rhinestones (earring is missing), c.1950s. $45-55 for the pair.

Bottom: Plastic earrings with heart shaped white on black plastic cameos depicting woman's portrait, c.1960s. $35-45.

Cameo earrings courtesy of Mary Liles.

Art plastic cameo brooch depicting woman set in gold metal frame with seed pearls. $55-65.
Courtesy of Nell Palmer Orr.

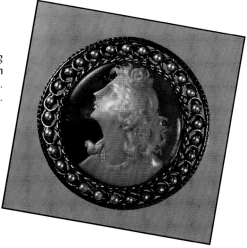

Necklace with jade stones and three cameos depicting woman's portrait, c.1950s. $98-128. *Courtesy of Mary Liles.*

Bakelite cameo depicting woman with flowers in her hair, set in gold metal frame decorated with Etruscan beading, c. 1940s. $95-125. *Courtesy of Mary Moon.*

White on pink plastic cameo brooch depicting woman, set in silver frame, c.1960s. $28-38. *Courtesy of Chaney Raley.*

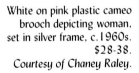

Metals

Top: 15-inch ribbon choker with glass cameo with gold metal rose and drop, c.1960s. $35-45.
Bottom: 5-inch Gold metal and rhinestone bracelet with three glass cameos with gold metal roses, c.1960s. $65-75.

Choker and bracelet courtesy of Shirley Ledbetter Jones.

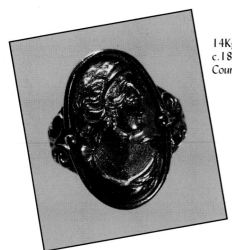

14Kgold ring depicting woman's portrait, c.1890s. $195-225.
Courtesy of Gayle Makowski.

Metal and rhinestones set with pendant, brooch, and pierced earrings, c.1990s. $195-225.
Courtesy of Teresa J. Rogers.

Silver metal brooch depicting cherub playing instrument, c. 1940s. $58-68. *Courtesy of Madonna Waller.*

Brooch with gold metal Gibson Girl cameo on black plastic, c. 1930s. $77-97. *Courtesy of Great Finds and Designs.*

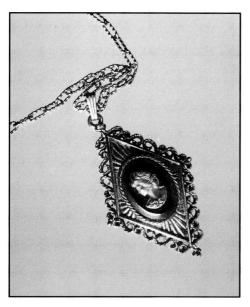

Gold metal pendant necklace with metal on black plastic cameo depicting woman's portrait. $48-58. *Courtesy of Mary Liles.*

153

Top: Metal intaglio brooch depicting woman's portrait, c.1950s. $47-58.
Bottom: Gold metal bracelet with cameo depicting woman's portrait, c.1980s. $55-65.

Bracelet and brooch courtesy of Teresa J. Rogers.

Copper relief depicting woman's portrait.
$30-40. *Courtesy of River City Cos.*

Metal cigarette case with portrait of woman adorned with flowers, c.1960s. $45-55. *Courtesy of Mary G. Moon.*

Glossary

Agate - A form of chalcedony with bands of color or irregular clouding.

Amber - A substance of brown, yellow, or orange fossil resin that is translucent and commonly found along the Baltic Shores.

Amethyst - A type of quartz that is transparent; it is purple or violet in color.

Art Deco - Refers to the period from 1910 through 1930 when an interest in the '20s centered around modern art movements. Angular lines in jewelry were popular at this time.

Art Nouveau - A period between 1890 to 1910 during which fluid lines were prominent in jewelry. Some popular motifs were dragonflies, mourning glories, and women depicted with long, flowing hair.

Bezel - A groove or flange that holds a piece in its setting.

Book Chain - A necklace made of links that was popular from the 1850s to the 1890s.

Bracelet - A piece of jewelry that encircles the wrist.

Brooch - A decorative pin.

Cameo - A portrait or scene that is carved in relief. Cameos have also been molded from glass and synthetics.

Cameo Habillé - A portrait adorned with jewelry such as a necklace and/or earrings and diadem.

Carnelian - A type of clear chalcedony that varies from pale to deep red or reddish brown.

Cast - A mold of an original piece done in plaster of paris.

Celluloid - Trademarked in 1869 by John Wesley Hyatt, this flammable material is colorless and made of nitrocellulose and camphor.

Chalcedony - A transparent quartz found in various colors, often in milky or gray.

Coral - Made by marine organisms called polyps which attach themselves to some object and eventually die leaving a skeleton behind. Over a period of years, the polyps form coral. Color ranges from pink to red as well as black and white.

Costume jewelry - Refers to the popular jewelry made of non-precious materials.

Crystal - A clear and transparent mineral that resembles ice.

Cut Steel - Beads resembling marcasites.

Diadem - A decorated headband that resembles a tiara.

Diamond - Extremely hard and valuable gem made of pure carbon, usually clear, but can be found in yellow, blue, black, or green.

Die Stamping - A process used in the mass production of jewelry in which a design is cut in metal.

Engraving - A method of cutting lines into metal.

Etruscan - Refers to a style of jewelry originated by the ancient Etruscans in Italy from the sixth and seventh centuries. The jewelry saw a revival in the nineteenth century. Patterns of gold beads on a gold background characterize Etruscan jewelry. Fornutato Pio Castellani, an Italian nineteenth-century jeweler, is given credit for reviving the Etruscan style of jewelry.

Faux - In French, this word means "false."

Filigree - A procedure in which fine wire has been twisted into a lace or web-like pattern.

Fob - Attached to a watch chain, this ornament was popular from the 1890s through the 1930s. Fobs experienced a revival with the renewed popularity of the pocket. Some fobs were set with intaglios or cameos.

Georgian - Refers to the period from 1714 to 1830 during which England was ruled by four of the Georges.

Gold-filled - Comprised of a base metal with an outer layer of gold.

Granulation - Decoration of a metal surface using tiny grains or gold beads. This process is characteristic of Etruscan jewelry, revived in the nineteenth century.

Gutta-percha - Made from the latex of tropical trees and used frequently during the nineteenth century.

Hallmark - A mark incised, stamped, or punched on silver or gold to show sterling or "carat" according to standards set by the country of origin. Some require other information such as manufacturer, patent, and origin.

Hematite - An iron ore that can be red or brown. The crystals are found mostly in men's jewelry.

High Relief - Used to describe a cameo in which the carving is raised to create a three-dimensional look.

Intaglio - A process opposite of cameo in which the artist carves into the stone below the surface.

Ivory - The yellowish, white, smooth substance that is hard and comes from the tusks of elephants. Often used to describe tusks from other animals or bone.

Jet - Used commonly in the nineteenth century, this substance was mined in Whitby, England, and was a type of fossilized coal.

Karat (Carat) - The weight of gems and gemstones or gold as set by a standard scale.

Lapis - A gemstone of deep blue that sometimes has small iron pyrite flecks.

Lava - A common substance for cameos in the early to late 1800s, lava from Pompeii ranged from a cream color, dark green, dark brown, black, and white. The softness of the material allowed carvers to create beautiful high relief carvings.

Locket - A piece of jewelry that functions as a pendant and/or a brooch and contains a compartment for a photograph or hair and a cover.

Lyre - Most closely associated with Apollo, this musical instrument resembles a harp.

Marcasite - A hard, white iron pyrite that is cut and set into Sterling silver.

Moonstone - A feldspar known for its pearly translucent color.

Mother-of-Pearl - The internal layer of mollusk shells that is iridescent in color.

Mounting - A backing or setting for a cameo or other pieces of jewelry.

Opal - A translucent and sometimes iridescent gem composed of hydrated silicon dioxide.

Parure - A set that commonly includes a necklace, earrings, brooches, and bracelets.

Pate-de-Verre - Heavy paste glass in muted colors; produced from crystal and lead that has been ground into paste, molded, and then fired in a kiln.

Pendant - A suspended piece of jewelry attached to a necklace or bracelet.

Pinchbeck - A substance made from an alloy of zinc to imitate gold. It was created by Christopher Pinchbeck (1670-1732), a London alchemist, jeweler, and watchmaker.

Plastic - Synthetic products made from chemicals which could be molded or carved into shapes and fashioned into jewelry. Early plastics proved impractical because of flammability, but celluloid was used during the Victorian Era, and Bakelite followed in the early 1900s.

Relief - The projection of a figure from a flat background.

Repoussé - A method of decorating metal where a design is pushed out on the back to stand out in relief on the front.

Rhinestone - A clear, imitation stone that has the sparkle of a diamond and is made of paste or glass.

Seed Pearl - A small pearl often used on frames of cameos.

Setting - A mounting for a cameo or other piece of jewelry.

Sterling silver - The highest standard of silver; it is 925 parts pure silver and 75 parts copper.

Stick Pin - A pin worn on a tie. It was popular with men from around 1870 to the early 1900s.

Topaz - An aluminum silicate mineral prized as a gemstone that varies in color from light yellow to deep orange.

Tortoiseshell - The covering of a sea turtle which is brown and translucent; used to make combs and jewelry.

Vermeil - Bronze, copper, or silver gilded and varnished to give a piece high luster. Usually a gold wash over silver.

Victorian Era - The years of Queen Victoria's reign (1837-1901).

Wedgwood - English firm began by Josiah Wedgwood. Through the production of jasparware in blues and whites or greens and whites, the company made hundreds of cameos, as well as cuff links, rings, tie pins (stickpins), and pendants. The motifs most often used were mythological.

Bibliography

Baker, Lillian. *100 Years of Collectible Jewelry*. Paducah, Kentucky: Collector Books, 1993.

Bell, Jeanenne. *Answers to Questions About Old Jewelry 1840-1950*. Florence, Alabama: Books Americana Inc., 1985.

Clements, Monica Lynn, and Patricia Rosser Clements. *Cameos: Classical to Costume*. Atglen, Pennsylvania: Schiffer Publishing, Ltd., 1998.

Darling, Ada. *Antique Jewelry*. Watkins Glen, New York: Century House, 1953.

Evans, Joan. *A History of Jewelry 1100-1870*. New York: Dover Publications, 1970.

Flower, Margaret. *Victorian Jewelry*. South Brunswick and New York: A.S. Barnes and Company, 1973.

Gere, Charlotte. *Victorian Jewelry Design*. Chicago: Henry Regnery Company, 1972.

Henig, Martin. *Classical Gems: Ancient and Modern Intaglios in Fitzwilliam Museum Cambridge*. Cambridge: Cambridge University Press, 1994.

Kaplan, Guy. *The Official Identification and Price Guide to Antique Jewelry*. New York: Random House, 1990.

Mastai, Marie-Louise d'Otrange. *Jewelry*. The Smithsonian Institution's National Museum of Design: Cooper-Hewitt Museum, 1981.

Miller, Anna M. *The Buyer's Guide to Affordable Antique Jewelry*. New York: Citadel Publishing Group, 1995.

Cameos Old and New. New York: Van Nostrand Reinhold, 1991.

Rowan, Michele. Nineteenth Century Cameos. Woodbridge, Suffolk: Antique Collectors Club, 2004

Sunderland, Beth Benton. *The Romance of Seals and Engraved Gems*. New York: The Macmillan Company, 1965.